"This book is a true contribution to guide the many significant others impacted by a family member's mental health struggles in a practical and constructive way. Families are often the unintended casualty of recovery avoidance, and are typically left feeling helpless and hopeless. Pollard and his skilled interdisciplinary team provide a step-by-step plan to empower significant others to choose behaviors that promote family well-being without blame or judgement. Congratulations!"

—**Barbara Van Noppen, PhD, LCSW**, clinical professor in psychiatry and the behavioral sciences at the Keck School of Medicine of the University of Southern California

"Recovery avoiders do NOT want to stay disabled. But they disappoint, inconvenience, and control their families in self-defeating ways. This is a sophisticated, compassionate, realistic look at how to improve the whole family's well-being. The authors describe gradually shifting from resentful accommodation and critical minimizing to incentivizing small, positive steps and refraining from unrealistic demands for change. Reducing the negative impact on the family ultimately opens the door to recovery."

—**Sally Winston**, founder and executive director of the Anxiety and Stress Disorders Institute (ASDI), and coauthor (with Martin Seif) of *Overcoming Unwanted Intrusive Thoughts*, *Needing to Know for Sure*, and *Overcoming Anticipatory Anxiety*

"If you've pleaded, nagged, and threatened your loved one to seek help for their mental health condition but they never do, then *When a Loved One Won't Seek Mental Health Treatment* is the book for you. It's filled with thoughtful and effective strategies to decrease family distress, encourage your loved one to seek help, and, more importantly, to help you live fully even when your loved one will not."

—**Michael A. Tompkins, PhD, ABPP**, codirector of the San Francisco Bay Area Center for Cognitive Therapy, and coauthor of *Digging Out*

"Pollard et al. have produced a family resource that explains the sufferer's issues without judgmental labels like resistant, controlling, etc. They replace such terminology with thoughtfully descriptive labels (e.g., recovery-avoidant behavior) and, more importantly, provide the reader with understandable reasons for why these behaviors occur. Understanding isn't a treatment program, but it is the foundation for any program that will be successful."

—**Jonathan B. Grayson, PhD**, licensed psychologist; director
of the Grayson LA Treatment Center for Anxiety and OCD;
and author of *Freedom from Obsessive Compulsive Disorder*,
as well as over four hundred articles and presentations

"This timely book draws on the authors' decades of experience working with families of people facing the most challenging behavioral health problems. It offers practical, step-by-step guidance on making changes that can help families be less controlled by their loved one's problems—and live healthier lives. Vignettes bring the strategies to life. I enthusiastically recommend this volume as a self-help resource, as well as to practicing therapists."

—**Debra A. Hope, PhD**, Aaron Douglas Professor of
Psychology at the University of Nebraska–Lincoln, and
lead author of *Managing Social Anxiety*

When a Loved One Won't Seek Mental Health Treatment

how to **promote recovery** and reclaim your family's well-being

C. Alec Pollard, PhD
Melanie VanDyke, PhD
Gary Mitchell, LCSW
Heidi J. Pollard, RN, MSN
Gloria Mathis, PhD

New Harbinger Publications, Inc.

Publisher's Note

NEW HARBINGER PUBLICATIONS is a registered trademark of New Harbinger Publications, Inc.

New Harbinger Publications is an employee-owned company.

Copyright © 2024 by C. Alec Pollard, Melanie VanDyke,
Gary Mitchell, Heidi J. Pollard, and Gloria Mathis
New Harbinger Publications, Inc.
5720 Shattuck Avenue
Oakland, CA 94609
www.newharbinger.com

Cover design by Amy Daniel

Acquired by Ryan Buresh

Edited by Kristi Hein

Library of Congress Cataloging-in-Publication Data on file

Printed in the United States of America

26   25   24

10   9   8   7   6   5   4   3   2   1   First Printing

Contents

Acknowledgments

This book would not have been possible without the many people who gave us support, encouragement, guidance, and input over the three decades during which the *family well-being approach* evolved. We are especially grateful to our colleagues, trainees, and students at the Saint Louis Behavioral Medicine Institute Center for OCD and Anxiety-Related Disorders. Their ideas and observations helped refine our thinking and the interventions we developed. We are thankful to Sue Mertens for her long-standing administrative support, and to Drs. Ronald Margolis and Jessica Gerfen, who, as leaders of the institution in which our approach was developed, steadfastly supported our efforts. We are, of course, grateful to the talented team at New Harbinger publications—Ryan Buresh, Vicraj Gill, Kristi Hein, Amy Shoup, and others—who helped us fine-tune the book's message. We also thank the International OCD Foundation for funding the initial study of our family consultation model that formed the basis for the family well-being approach.

C. Alec Pollard: First and foremost, I thank my wife and coauthor, Heidi—my perpetual source of inspiration, encouragement, intellectual stimulation, and, as much as it pains me to admit it, useful criticism. I'm grateful to my son, Matt, for understanding when writing obligations diverted me from family events, and for always being interested in what I was up to. I thank my three precious grandchildren, Ethan, Isaac, and Mila, just for being themselves, and for reliably enticing "Bop-Bop" to forget about work and have some play time.

Melanie VanDyke: I would like to acknowledge everyone who has supported the development of the family well-being approach. My former students—especially Taylor Washington, Angel John, and Jacob Harper, and colleagues, especially Kami Hancock and Susan Mueller—provided helpful notes to make our book more accessible and welcoming. I also thank Valerie Baker, for sharing her expertise on financial planning resources. Most of all,

I appreciate Chris, Jared, and Leo (as well as our family and friends)—your loving support and good cheer have sustained me throughout the research and writing process.

Gary Mitchell: I want to thank my wife, Essie, for her patience with my numerous "writing weekends" away from home. And for her willingness to help me edit, and re-edit, so many early drafts. And to both of my sons, Mayer and Solomon, for their encouragement and their intellectual curiosity.

Heidi J. Pollard: To my husband, Alec, who helped keep all of us on track, I always knew you could do it, my love. To my son, Matt, the center of my life: Thank you for your support and encouragement. To my grandchildren, Ethan, Isaac, and Mila, who insist I be first in line to pick them up from school: Thanks for all the joy you bring to my world.

Gloria Mathis: I'd like to thank my parents for helping me believe I could do anything I wanted to do, and making it possible, in all ways, to pursue this path for my life. Thank you to the many mentors who have supported me throughout my educational and professional career. I also want to thank my friend and business partner, Dr. Jennifer Kessler, for encouraging me to strive for more and understanding when I needed to prioritize my book obligations.

Last but not least, we are immeasurably grateful to the many families with whom we have had the privilege to work. We thank them for all they have taught us and for their patience as we discovered how to escape the family trap. It is to them this book is dedicated.

Foreword

I'm delighted to see the decades of thoughtful work of Dr. Alec Pollard and his colleagues come to fruition in this book for families whose loved one has been avoiding working on their mental health problems. Dr. Pollard has been a wonderful colleague to many of us clinicians and researchers who work with obsessive-compulsive and related disorders. He is a consummate clinician and outstanding trainer and coordinator of trainings in obsessive-compulsive disorder (OCD) and other mental health problems. Over the years, Pollard and his interdisciplinary team of dedicated collaborators—including Melanie VanDyke; his wife, Heidi Pollard; Gary Mitchell; and Gloria Mathis—have helped the families of loved ones evading recovery from a variety of mental health conditions.

Recognition of the need to help these families developed directly from the team's clinical work. We who work in similar clinical mental health fields understood the challenge all too well, as we received calls from family members seeking referrals and asking how they could convince their loved one to make the call and attend treatment sessions. Family members had done their homework. They knew there were well-established, effective treatments for their relative's condition. Why wouldn't their loved one agree to engage in therapy that would surely help? Understandably, family members were frustrated and often angry that their loved one would not take the basic steps needed to resolve their own problem. Unfortunately, many family members had been accommodating their loved one's unreasonable requests, further worsening the family situation.

The effort to find an answer gained steam when Pollard and his colleagues received a competitive grant from the International OCD Foundation to develop and test an intervention program aimed at helping families in this situation. The research that evolved, spearheaded by Dr. Melanie VanDyke, provided the foundation for development of the family well-being approach and the writing of this important book.

The book's definition of recovery avoidance—"recurrent failure to explore, pursue, or take advantage of resources and opportunities available for resolving problems or improving health or functioning"—captures a range of problems that frustrate family members, including outright denial, insistence that the problem isn't their own, failure to seek help, seeking the wrong kind of help, and/or finding help but not doing the work. What might help ease the family burden and corresponding family conflict over these issues?

Pollard and colleagues' family well-being approach arose from decades of effort to help families escape the trap their loved one's recovery avoidance imposes on the family. In this book they clarify what causes recovery avoidance and offer specific strategies for developing and implementing plans to move forward in these tough family situations. The book is an easy and heartening read that lifts the spirit. The language is clear and nonjudgmental, spawned from the basic premise that no one wants to have mental health problems or have those problems interfere with their own or their family's enjoyment of life. The step-by-step approach taught in this book is based in well-established ways to influence human behavior. Many examples of family behaviors are offered and expanded in the final section on Family Stories. Especially important are the very practical descriptions and recommendations for next steps that enable a family member to create a plan and follow it to improve their own and their family's well-being. And the delightfully clear recommendations for obtaining help from professionals are especially useful, given the limited number of clinicians with expertise in either the specific mental health problem the family faces or in helping families, versus individual clients/patients, deal with such problems.

Congratulations to the authors for developing this user-friendly family plan to encourage family self-care and help-seeking behavior in reluctant relatives with mental health problems.

—Gail Steketee, PhD
Professor and Dean Emerita,
Boston University School of Social Work

Introduction

Olivia paused longer than usual at the door. She didn't want to go inside. She remembered how things used to be, when she looked forward to coming home, before her brother, Robert, changed. She shook her head, opened the door, and walked directly to the designated bathroom, where she undressed and stepped into the shower. Afterward, she put on specially cleaned clothes hung by the shower door.

In the kitchen, Olivia's mother was decorating a birthday cake. It was Olivia's fourteenth birthday. But there would be no big celebration today. No friends would be coming over, because Robert fears they'd bring contamination into the house. Olivia knows her brother has OCD, but she can't help feeling resentful, wondering why she has to sacrifice so much because of his problem.

Olivia doesn't have OCD, but she suffers from it nonetheless. And she's not alone. The lives of countless family members are disrupted every day by a loved one's mental illness—including the families we'll be referring to throughout this book:

- Sara's husband is severely depressed. He sleeps most of the day and doesn't work, leaving Sara overwhelmed by the household and financial responsibilities her husband no longer assumes.

- Vivienne, Amy, and Andrew's mother has a hoarding problem. They monitor her safety and spend countless hours cleaning up the clutter and hazardous conditions their mother lives in.

- Cathy's teenage daughter, Caitlyn, has severe social anxiety. Every morning is a major battle, as Cathy tries to get her child to school, often late or not at all.

- Roy's wife, Lynn, worries a lot about the many physical symptoms she experiences. Her quest to find a medical explanation has left

Roy overwhelmed with medical bills and his two daughters resentful that "Mom's not there for us like she used to be."

- Rachel—whose husband, Sam, fears he'll make a mistake that will cause harm to others—is often late to work and sometimes misses appointments altogether because so much of her time is spent reassuring her husband and helping him double-check things around the house.

Mental health is truly a family affair. Any disorder, any level of impairment, can disturb the family environment, and, in many cases, the impact is devastating. The struggles of one family member can compromise the physical, psychological, social, and financial stability of the entire family (Fekadu et al. 2019).

For most families, hope rests on the promise of treatment. And there's good reason to have hope. Evidence-based psychotherapies, medication, or some combination of both have helped millions of individuals recapture their lives and those of their families as well. On top of that, promising new therapies are being investigated every day.

There's just one problem. Even the best treatment doesn't work if it's never received.

In fact, at least half the people suffering from mental and emotional disorders don't receive the help they need (Substance Abuse and Mental Health Services Administration 2022). Some lack access. But even when effective treatment's available, there are many who refuse to go, promise to go but never do, or show up but never really participate. As you'll learn, these folks are what we call *recovery avoiders*. We use this term to highlight the effect of a person's behavior, not their intention. Recovery avoiders don't set out to become disabled, nor do they intend to disrupt their family's lives. Recovery avoidance simply describes a pattern of behavior that's incompatible with recovery. There are real reasons your loved one avoids recovery— like misinformed beliefs, skill deficits, competing incentives, and deficiencies in motivation—but none involve a desire or decision to remain impaired. We'll explore the causes of recovery avoidance more in chapter 1.

Regardless of what's behind the behavior, recovery avoidance presents another layer of burden for families. Without hope of treatment, there's little reason to expect things to improve. It's natural to feel disheartened about the future when you're in a situation like this—to feel resentment and anger when someone you love appears to be doing nothing about a problem that's causing so much distress for everyone involved. And when family members feel it's their responsibility to save their loved one, they endure the added burden of guilt over what they unjustifiably perceive as their own failure. Caring for someone who's experiencing mental health difficulties can be hard enough, but it's even harder when the person you love is avoiding recovery.

Whether it's your son, daughter, partner, spouse, parent, or other family member, when a loved one avoids recovery and doesn't do the things you believe could improve their quality of life, it's hard not to lose hope. And when your well-being is tethered to someone else's behavior, someone who's unwilling or unable to change, you're likely to feel trapped. That's the fundamental dilemma of families grappling with recovery avoidance. They're stuck in what we call the *family trap*, because their hope for the future rests largely on another person's behavior. And despite multiple failed attempts to change that person, families keep trying the same tactics, over and over, with little or nothing to show for it. They know it's not working, but they don't know what else to do. They're stuck.

The Family's Futile Quest for Help

Those stuck in the family trap need help, but there's no one there to provide it. Some families reach out to a clinician, but unfortunately that doesn't always go so well, like when Sara tried to get help for her depressed husband:

Sara: My husband's severely depressed. He really needs help.

Dr. Typical: Is there a reason your husband didn't call me himself?

Sara: He doesn't believe treatment will help. He says it's a waste of time. But he doesn't leave the house and rarely gets out of bed.

Dr. Typical: Sounds like he's depressed, all right, but there's nothing I can do unless he wants help.

Sara: So that's it? You won't help us?

Dr. Typical: I'm sorry. But have your husband call me if he changes his mind.

Sadly, Sara's experience is typical. And before we, as therapists ourselves, started working with families, we were much like Dr. Typical. After all, therapists know they're not magicians. How can they treat a person who doesn't want help? Even if Sara pressured her husband into therapy, working with a coerced patient is usually unpleasant and almost always unproductive. Still, there's something Dr. Typical could've done to be more helpful. The mistake was not refusing to treat the person who didn't want help. It was ignoring the person who did.

Rethinking How to Help Families

It never felt right to leave families in such an untenable position, but for a long time we simply didn't realize there was anything else to be done. We thought our sole responsibility was to treat the person with a mental health problem, and if they weren't receptive, there was no other option. Sure, we routinely included families in treatment sessions, but the identified patient was present, and their disorder was the primary focus. It never occurred to us to conduct therapy without "the patient," instead focusing on the rest of the family. We were as stuck in our way of thinking as those families were stuck in recovery avoidance.

Eventually, our view of the problem changed. Families taught us how to understand their dilemma. They shared their daily struggles, how they felt abandoned by health care professionals and blamed for their loved one's failure to recover. We realized the magnitude of disruption so many families experience. If our job is to treat mental illness, shouldn't that include all who suffer? Other family members were struggling; they deserved our help too. At the very least, we could teach families how to lessen the impact of recovery avoidance on their own lives.

We also recognized that our knowledge of motivation was being used only to decide who *not* to help. Like most traditional therapists, we knew the futility of treating an individual who isn't motivated to change. That part of our clinical judgment was reasonable. But we were ignoring those motivated family members. Unlike the recovery avoider, they wanted help.

Finally, we realized that certain family interactions are more than just ineffective. Sometimes they make things worse. Families don't cause mental illness, but they can influence the course of a disorder. We knew from clinical observation, and subsequently from emerging research (Butzlaff and Hooley 1998), that certain family patterns are associated with more severe impairment and poorer response to treatment. By not providing guidance to these families, we were failing to give them the opportunity to create a family environment that better facilitates recovery.

As we adopted this new perspective, we began exploring ways to help families. In the early 1990s there were no manuals or workbooks on this topic, but there were resources to draw on. We investigated how recovery avoidance was addressed in the field of alcohol and drug dependence, and we recognized some of those concepts and interventions might be helpful for the families we were seeing. We studied family systems theory, which helped us understand how families become locked into patterns of dysfunctional behavior, and how we might help unlock those patterns. We were also heavily influenced by cognitive behavior therapy (CBT), a type of psychotherapy successfully applied to a variety of problems involving anxiety, depression, guilt, and anger—the very emotions that can hinder families trying to escape the family trap. Additionally, CBT provides effective strategies to generate behavior change, a crucial ingredient for achieving family well-being.

This book is the culmination of three decades of work by the Family Consultation Team at Saint Louis Behavioral Medicine Institute and Saint Louis University School of Medicine. It describes a new approach to recovery avoidance, one that promises hope for the many families struggling to escape the family trap.

About This Book

The method described in this book is called the *family well-being approach.* As you'll discover, our approach prioritizes the emotional health of the entire family. Promoting family well-being is critical, because most people stuck in the family trap are trying to help their loved one under suboptimal conditions—while living in a distressed family environment. That's a big reason they continue to struggle. It's like trying to tread water with an anvil strapped to your back. In this book, we'll help you remove the anvil. That means learning how to ease distress within your family—and knowing why it's so important to do so. It means learning how to reverse recovery avoidance and get your loved one on the path to functioning better. But first, it means becoming emotionally and strategically prepared to do all of this effectively. We'll help you help your loved one—but, as we've learned, that rarely happens when the welfare of the rest of the family is overlooked. First things first.

Who Might Benefit from This Book

It was the plight of families grappling with untreated OCD that first captured our attention, but we soon realized the interventions we were using could benefit families dealing with a variety of conditions. Over the years, we've helped the families of individuals diagnosed with panic disorder, agoraphobia, social anxiety disorder, generalized anxiety disorder, separation anxiety disorder, posttraumatic stress disorder, major depression, body dysmorphic disorder, illness anxiety disorder, borderline personality disorder, hoarding disorder, and various eating disorders. In many cases, the family's loved one had received multiple diagnoses. We've not tested our method with every possible disorder. However, the potential benefit of our approach may have more to do with the nature of the family situation than the specific disorder involved. The families we've helped have had five characteristics in common:

- Someone in the family was behaviorally impaired by a mental disorder.

- The loved one with the disorder was a recovery avoider.

- The loved one's state of impairment created distress or disruption in the lives of other family members.

- The family's efforts to change the loved one had failed.

- At least one family member was willing to try a new approach.

If these characteristics describe your family situation, please read on.

How the Book Is Organized

The book is organized into two main parts that tell you what you need to know (part 1) and what you need to do (part 2) to improve your family's well-being.

PART 1, THE FAMILY TRAP: WHAT YOU NEED TO KNOW

Here we describe the dilemmas that families face when dealing with a loved one who doesn't seek recovery. In chapter 1, we discuss the concept of *recovery avoidance* and explain why some people act in ways inconsistent with recovery. Chapter 2 describes the ways in which families naturally respond when someone they care about is a recovery avoider. We introduce the concepts of *accommodation* and *minimization*—two common, but counterproductive forms of family behavior that can make recovery avoidance worse—and we describe how accommodation, minimization, and recovery avoidance interact to create the family trap. In chapter 3, we describe a way out of the trap: the family well-being approach. Chapter 4 alerts you to common obstacles you might encounter as you follow the steps outlined in part 2, and suggests ways to overcome those obstacles.

PART 2, ESCAPING THE FAMILY TRAP: WHAT YOU NEED TO DO

In this part, we describe the five steps of pursuing family well-being using the family well-being approach:

- **Step 1** (chapters 5 and 6) helps you anticipate and plan for potential crises—in particular, the troublesome and potentially dangerous ways your loved one might resist the changes you plan to make.

- **Step 2** helps you identify areas of your life that've been negatively affected by your loved one's condition (chapter 7). It also assists you to prioritize the changes you most want to make (chapter 8).

- **Step 3** is for family members who, in dealing with recovery avoidance, have abandoned activities they value. Chapters 9 and 10 are designed to help you get those activities back into your life.

- **Step 4** (chapters 11 and 12) is for families who want to ease family distress and improve the quality of interactions with their loved one. This step helps you organize and implement a plan to replace counterproductive behavior with more effective approaches to recovery avoidance.

- **Step 5** (chapters 13 and 14) teaches you how to promote healthy behavior in your loved one. You'll learn strategies that discourage recovery avoidance and encourage recovery behavior, while avoiding power struggles.

ADDITIONAL MATERIALS

The final chapter (chapter 15) outlines three additional steps you may need to consider beyond the five main steps of the family well-being approach—specifically, it helps you decide when it's necessary to remove a foundational accommodation (an accommodation your loved one depends on as a basic necessity, like food or shelter), whether and how to get professional consultation, and the extent to which you should plan for the road ahead to safeguard the future of your loved one and the family as a whole.

In the back of the book, after chapter 15, are three additional sections. "Family Stories" provides information on each of the six families we feature in this book. After that, a "Glossary" revisits and defines all the key terms you need to know to follow the family well-being approach. Finally, the references document cites research findings, other books, and journal articles. Throughout the book, we'll refer to online resources (http://www.newharbinger.com/53134) where you can access worksheets and other information relevant to achieving family well-being.

A Few Cautions Before You Begin

Before moving on to chapter 1, three cautions. First, please don't skip steps that might be valuable to you. Doing so could jeopardize your preparation for subsequent steps. The main reason families remain entangled in the web of recovery avoidance is not that they don't know what to do, but that they act before they are emotionally and strategically prepared. Every family will need steps 1 and 2. For steps 3 through 5, use the "Precheck" at the beginning of each step to help you determine whether that step is relevant to your situation.

Second, keep in mind, our book isn't a substitute for professional guidance. Some families may able to use this book successfully on their own, but others will benefit from additional assistance. We discuss the prospect of working with a professional in chapter 15. However, if at any point you feel discouraged or stuck in your efforts to improve your family's well-being, please consult a licensed mental health professional. Our book can help guide your therapist's efforts to assist you.

Finally, tension in families dealing with recovery avoidance can easily escalate and, in some cases, endanger family members. The family well-being approach looks at the big picture, the long-term consequences of grappling with recovery avoidance, and how to free yourself from counterproductive family interactions. Helping you anticipate potential crises is part of our approach, but it isn't addressed until chapters 5 and 6. If an incident arises before then, please take whatever action you feel is necessary to ensure your family's safety and welfare.

Moving Forward

In chapter 1 we'll dive deeper into the nature of recovery avoidance—what it is, why it happens, and what perpetuates it. From there, we'll begin to explore how you might help your loved one and your whole family turn things around. We hope you find this book helpful, and we wish you all the best as you seek to improve your family's well-being.

PART 1

The Family Trap: What You Need to Know

In part 1, you'll learn what's happened to your family and why. The concepts and principles you'll learn in part 1 provide the groundwork you need to advance to part 2, where you'll learn what you need to do to improve your family's well-being.

CHAPTER 1

The Nature of Recovery Avoidance

Main Point: In this chapter, you'll learn the meaning of recovery avoidance and the reasons people behave in ways that are incompatible with recovery.

It's common for people to behave in ways inconsistent with their self-interest. Most of us have struggled to follow a healthy diet, exercise regularly, drop a bad habit, or get the proper amount of sleep. And flossing your teeth daily? Not even a third of us do that. Human behavior is not always rational, healthy, or constructive. What's more, self-improvement typically means adopting new behavior—which sometimes involves more work, discomfort, or inconvenience than we're willing to tolerate.

Redirecting behavior in a healthy direction can be hard for anyone, and especially difficult for someone dealing with mental illness—a challenge no one chooses to have. Keep these points in mind. It will help you better understand recovery avoidance and optimize empathy for the loved one whose condition prompted you to read this book.

Defining Recovery Avoidance

Recovery is the process of gaining a better emotional or physical state of health or functioning; avoidance is the act of keeping away from something. If we put these concepts together, recovery avoidance can be defined as the act of keeping away from a process that will lead to improved health or functioning. A complete definition, however, should include two additional points. First, recovery avoidance is a pattern of behavior that develops over time, not a momentary lapse. Second, recovery avoidance is more than the absence of improvement; it's active failure to take advantage of resources and opportunities that could lead to improvement.

Therefore we define recovery avoidance as *recurrent failure to explore, pursue, or take advantage of resources and opportunities available for resolving problems or improving health or functioning.*

Ultimately, a person can avoid any aspect of health or well-being. In this book, our focus is on those who avoid recovery from psychiatric and behavioral impairment—something we first wrote about over two decades ago (Pollard and Pollard 2002). Recovery avoidance can be expressed in a variety of ways. Some people deny having a problem. Others acknowledge a problem but insist it's not psychiatric. Some acknowledge having a psychiatric disorder but never seek help. Others continually seek the wrong kind of help. And some find the right help, perhaps at the insistence of others, but, sadly, never seem to take advantage of it. In each of these examples of recovery avoidance, the individual's behavior is incompatible with the pursuit of recovery.

How does the loved one in your life express recovery avoidance? Take a moment to think about this before you read on.

Common Misconceptions About Recovery Avoidance

It's natural to wonder why anyone wouldn't do everything possible to overcome a problem, especially one associated with significant suffering. Family members, understandably frustrated with the situation, sometimes think of recovery avoidance as their loved one's willful choice to be impaired. They may view their loved one as lazy, unmotivated, selfish, spoiled, or oppositional. If you've felt this way about someone in your family, it's understandable, especially if you've had no other way to make sense of their behavior. But be careful. Negative labels tell us nothing about why someone avoids recovery, much less what to do about it. More important, this kind of negative judgment can fuel your anger and compel you to interact with your loved one in counterproductive ways. Fortunately, the science of human behavior offers a much more useful way to understand recovery avoidance.

The Real Reasons People Avoid Recovery

Four factors can contribute to recovery avoidance: recovery-interfering beliefs, skill deficits, motivation deficits, and incentive deficits. In the sections that follow, we'll dive into each factor. As you read, keep in mind, we're not talking about what causes an individual's psychiatric disorder, since everyone with a mental illness isn't a recovery avoider. We're talking specifically about factors that underlie recovery avoidance.

Recovery-Interfering Beliefs

Beliefs affect behavior, and certain beliefs get in the way of recovery. For example, people who believe they don't have a problem or that their condition is untreatable are unlikely to seek professional help. When strongly held beliefs like this become highly rigid, they're called *overvalued ideation*. People with overvalued ideation are particularly vulnerable to recovery avoidance. They may be perfectly reasonable in other areas of their life, but when you attempt to discuss beliefs related to their recovery avoidance, they lack insight and are unreceptive when their beliefs are challenged.

Malik knows he has a problem with anxiety, but he firmly believes medication would "poison my body." Whenever his family urges him to talk to his doctor, he becomes angry and accuses his family of endangering his life. Malik is unlikely to try something he believes is poison—and his family's been unable to convince him otherwise.

Skill Deficits

Certain skills are necessary for recovery behavior. The seemingly simple act of finding a qualified provider, for example, involves the ability to: (1) investigate options, (2) make decisions, (3) develop a plan, and (4) follow through with the plan. Not everyone does this well. Other kinds of skill deficits can contribute to recovery avoidance; for example, the inability to tolerate negative emotions. A person without this skill might be driven to avoid anything that might involve the experience of uncomfortable feelings, including psychotherapy.

> *Jenny is poorly organized and puts things off. When her family suggests she get help, she tells them she will, but she never follows through. The thought of planning where and how to get help seems overwhelming. She struggles even to set up an initial appointment. I'll do it tomorrow, she tells herself, but she can't seem to make it happen.*

Motivation Deficits

Motivation is the desire to act in service of a goal. The goal of getting a raise, for example, can create a desire to work hard. People motivated to seek recovery also have goals. They want to graduate from school, find a job, get married, or learn to drive a car. And when they see their psychiatric impairment as an obstacle to achieving their goals, they'll be motivated to do the things necessary to get better. But what if the impaired individual doesn't have goals or doesn't view their impairment as an obstacle? That person will lack the desire necessary to seek recovery.

> *Sidney is twenty-four but doesn't seem to have career aspirations or any other identifiable long-term goal. He expresses little interest in having a family or becoming self-reliant. He lacks the kinds of goals that would motivate him to pursue recovery.*

Incentive Deficits

Human behavior is also influenced by what happens right after a behavior occurs. While motivation is fueled by the desired long-term consequences of behavior—the eventual outcome you believe certain behaviors will help you achieve—incentives are the more immediate, short-term consequences. Incentives, which emerge from our environment, involve either experiencing something rewarding (money, privilege, approval from others, pleasant feelings) or escaping something punishing (loss of money or privileges, disapproval from others, unpleasant feelings). An incentive deficit exists when the incentives to avoid recovery are more influential than the incentives to seek recovery.

> *Sofia's twenty-eight but doesn't work and hardly leaves the house. Her parents provide food, a place to live, and internet so "she can connect with her friends." Unlike Sidney, Sofia has goals. She wants to become an architect and get her own place. But the very thought of this makes her anxious. It's easier to put school off and play video games instead. Sofia's environment incentivizes recovery avoidance and inadequately promotes recovery behavior.*

In summary, people don't engage in recovery avoidance because they're lazy or willful. They do so because of their counterproductive beliefs, the skills they lack, the motivation they're missing, or the disincentives they face. Any one of these four factors can generate a pattern of recovery avoidance.

Moving Forward

Now that you've read a bit more about recovery avoidance, how do you see your loved one and your family's situation? Hopefully, you now have a more useful way of thinking about recovery avoidance. You realize that your loved one has not willfully chosen a life of disability. You've learned that recovery avoidance is driven by one or more powerful factors that compel individuals to avoid recovery—the same factors that can make all of us behave in ways contrary to our own self-interest. Recognizing what truly drives recovery avoidance can promote empathy for your loved one and, ultimately, help you change how you approach the problem. But first, there's more for you to learn. In the next chapter, you'll discover some things that might at first be uncomfortable to think about: how you might be contributing to the problem. Understanding your role in recovery avoidance is the key to escaping the family trap.

CHAPTER 2

The Family's Role in Recovery Avoidance

Main Point: You'll learn about two common but counterproductive ways families respond to a loved one who's avoiding recovery: accommodating and minimizing. These two responses interact with recovery avoidance to create what we call the family trap.

Few, if any, of us are prepared to respond effectively to recovery avoidance. There are no courses in school to teach us how to deal with an impaired relative, much less with someone who's a recovery avoider. When confronted with recovery avoidance, families do the best they can with what they know to do. And what they do is remarkably consistent across families, because most families respond intuitively, out of a natural desire to help a loved one who's suffering. One family member needs help; another is trying to provide it. What could possibly go wrong? As we've learned from decades of research, the answer is: plenty.

How Things Go Wrong

Research on *expressed emotion* (EE) tells us that how families respond to psychiatric impairment matters a lot. EE refers to aspects of the family environment—in part a reflection of the attitudes of family members—that can unintentionally worsen an individual's condition. These attitudes get conveyed in the form of critical comments, expressions of frustration or hostility, and overinvolvement in the impaired loved one's problem. Investigations of family interaction find that high levels of EE are associated with greater symptom severity and increased likelihood of relapse (Butzlaff and Hooley 1998; Wearden et al. 2000).

How families respond to a psychiatric disorder makes a big difference, particularly when recovery avoidance is involved. And families confronted with recovery avoidance are especially vulnerable to EE. If your loved one is a recovery avoider, things seem to go wrong no matter what you do. If you try making life easier for them, you wind up perpetuating dependency and entitlement. If you push them to seek recovery, you're met with resistance or outright hostility. You're between a rock and a hard place.

Take a moment to think about your experience trying to help the recovery avoider in your life. What happens when you try to help them? How do they respond, and how do you feel when this happens?

There are two critical sides of a family's response to recovery avoidance:

- *Accommodation*—the emotional and behavioral overinvolvement in a recovery avoider's life that fosters dependency and reinforces avoidance

- *Minimization*—the negative interactions with a recovery avoider that generate defensiveness and accelerate family conflict (Pollard and Pollard 2006)

Both are natural responses to a situation that can be profoundly stressful. But both are ineffective and often make things worse. The result is a perpetual escalation of unhappiness, dysfunction, and conflict within the family—the family trap.

Waiting for your loved one to "get it" doesn't work. To escape the trap, you'll need to take a hard look at how you respond to them: in particular, how you accommodate and minimize. And you'll need to be willing to consider the alternative approach this book teaches. But before you learn what to do, you need to be clear about what *not* to do, and why.

The Two Counterproductive Responses to Recovery Avoidance

It bears repeating: The natural response to recovery avoidance is to try to help your loved one. Families initially provide assistance and encouragement to promote a loved one's comfort or functioning. Unfortunately, when recovery avoidance is involved, assistance becomes accommodating, and encouragement devolves into minimizing.

Accommodation

The term *accommodation* originally emerged from observations of families dealing with a loved one struggling with OCD. It refers to the way family members adapt to the disorder by joining in compulsions, helping the OCD sufferer avoid anxiety-provoking situations, and otherwise altering family routines. Accommodation is an understandable response to OCD for a family member trying to lessen a loved one's discomfort or impairment. Nonetheless, it perpetuates their condition.

Today, we recognize that accommodations are not restricted to OCD. They can occur in families dealing with a variety of psychiatric disorders (Lebowitz, Panza, and Bloch 2016; Shimshoni, Shrinivasa, Cherian, and Lebowitz 2019). Any behavior intended to assist, appease, give in to, or compensate for an impaired individual can be considered accommodation. The term *enabling* is sometimes used to describe the same concept.

There are two kinds of accommodation:

- *Accommodations of omission* are the *things you give up.* They're the valued activities you've dropped or neglected to pursue because of your loved one. Examples: no longer entertaining guests at home, giving up favorite leisure activities, quitting your job.

- *Accommodations of commission* are the *things you take on* in response to an impaired individual's limitations or demands—things you typically wouldn't do for a person who wasn't impaired. Examples: doing your child's homework, performing your spouse's responsibilities, repeatedly providing reassurance, walking on eggshells to avoid upsetting someone.

Although it's important to recognize the detrimental effects of accommodation, let's pause to recognize its positive side. Accommodating another person is normally considered an act of kindness, generosity, or good service.

Accommodations are modifications we make to work, school, and other environments, in light of people's differing needs, to ensure a level playing field for all. They're the means by which the Americans with Disabilities Act protects disabled individuals from discrimination. Schools accommodate when they give students who need extra time to take tests, and businesses accommodate when they adjust work conditions to assist an employee with particular needs. These are all good things.

Families grappling with recovery avoidance also intend to do good things. They want to help someone they care about; to shield that person from distress or assist the person to get something done; to avoid conflict and keep peace in the family. In short, there are good reasons for one person to accommodate another. But there are even better reasons *not* to accommodate when the person being accommodated is avoiding recovery. When families first begin to accommodate, they don't realize they're stepping into the family trap. They've yet to grasp the long-term consequences of their actions and what's about to happen to their lives.

Now let's reexamine the dark side of accommodating and why it's particularly harmful to accommodate a recovery avoider. First, accommodations foster dependency, depriving your loved one of opportunities to learn and accomplish something. The underlying message of accommodating is "you're incapable of doing this on your own." More important, accommodating shields them from the natural consequences of their disorder—the very consequences needed to help them recognize the severity of their problem and create the desire to seek help. People don't typically call their doctor, reach out for help, or change what they've been doing unless they experience negative consequences—like feeling pain or being unable to do something they want to do. If you're helping shield your loved one from the natural consequences of their disorder, you've unwittingly become an additional barrier between them and the pursuit of recovery. Despite your good intentions, you've become an accomplice to recovery avoidance. Clinical studies indicate that higher levels of family accommodation are associated with greater symptom severity and poorer response to treatment (Shimshoni, Shrinivasa, Cherian, and Lebowitz 2019).

Second, accommodation jeopardizes *your* emotional health as well (Lebowitz, Panza, and Bloch 2016). The family trap is a toxic environment. Accommodations of commission deplete you, and accommodations of omission deprive you of opportunities to replenish. You're doing things you don't want to do and not doing things you'd like to do—because of someone else's problem. Maintaining accommodations for any length of time can easily lead to frustration, resentment, fatigue, and, eventually, burnout. And that means you're less equipped to deal effectively with your loved one and more prone to engage in a second kind of counterproductive behavior—*minimization*.

Before reading on, consider how you accommodate your loved one. You'll have time to consider this in more detail later in the book; for now, just give the matter some thought. Understanding how you accommodate and why it's counterproductive is critical for you to escape the family trap.

Minimization

Minimization is defined as persistent and ineffective behavior, verbal or otherwise, intended to influence a person with a psychiatric disorder to change. We selected the term *minimizing* to emphasize the flawed assumption underlying the behavior—that the person avoiding recovery will change because of something the minimizer says, does, rejects, or withholds. Examples of minimizing behavior include lecturing, nagging, yelling, pleading, criticizing, prodding, or any other behavior designed to get psychiatrically impaired individuals to do something they're unable or unwilling to do.

The implicit message of minimizing is "you can and should change now"—a message that trivializes the magnitude of the challenge your loved one is facing. You may not realize it at the time, but when you minimize, you're failing to recognize the strength of the forces that drive recovery avoidance. And that failure is being communicated to your loved one. The message they receive is that you believe they have the ability to simply snap out of it. In fact, they don't know how to change and certainly can't do so on command.

Minimizing often involves overtly critical or hostile behavior, but not always. A family member might calmly recite the reasons their loved one ought to seek help, without any overt sign of negative emotion—but if the underlying objective is to change them, and you keep repeating the behavior despite the fact that it doesn't work, you're minimizing.

By now, we hope you recognize that minimizing won't generate the outcome you desire. Loved ones avoiding recovery don't change for the better because their families lecture or criticize them. The fact that it doesn't work is reason enough to stop minimizing. But there's an even better reason—it makes things worse.

Like accommodation, minimizing contributes to recovery avoidance. Instead of motivating the pursuit of recovery, it weakens your loved one's desire to try. The implicit message of minimizing ("you can and should change now") is experienced as pressure, which heightens their fear. It also reinforces their perception that you don't understand what they're going through, which is likely to create distrust and anger. Fear, distrust, and anger won't spur them to change. Quite the opposite: They create defensiveness, which ultimately leads to more recovery avoidance.

Minimizing has a negative impact on you as well. Because things usually don't end well, you're likely to feel bad afterward. Let's face it: When we criticize or nag or lecture, it's usually not our finest hour. You may feel guilty or ashamed because you said or did something you regret. You may feel frustrated because nothing changed, or resentful about how your loved one treated you. Any one of these negative reactions can cloud your judgment and provide the emotional justification for continued minimizing, which simply leads you further into the family trap.

Are there ways you've responded to your loved one that qualify as minimizing? Again, take a moment to think about it before you read on. Try to be honest with yourself. Minimizing may not always be pretty, but it's a natural part of the family trap.

The Family Trap

Now that you understand the concepts of recovery avoidance, accommodating, and minimizing, let's examine how the three interact to create the family trap, as illustrated in the diagram. Don't be intimidated by all the arrows and boxes. We'll walk you through how it all works.

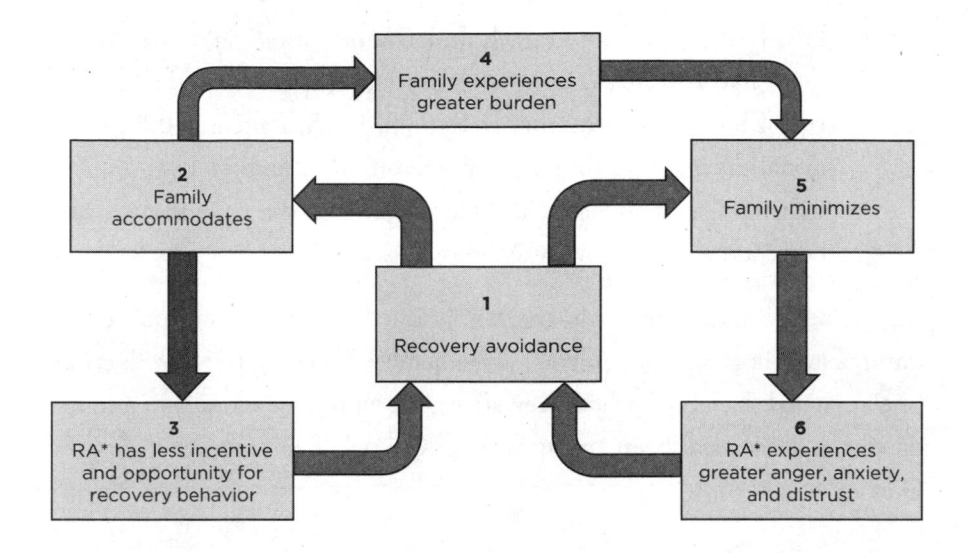

*RA = recovery avoider

Diagram 1: The Family Trap

The "Family Trap" diagram illustrates three important chains of events:

- First (boxes 1, 2, and 3), the vicious cycle of recovery avoidance and accommodation. Recovery avoidance (box 1) provokes the family to accommodate (box 2), which in turn blunts the natural consequences of the disorder (box 3), which reduces the recovery avoider's incentive to pursue recovery and thus perpetuates recovery avoidance (box 1). The more you accommodate, the more your loved one avoids recovery. And the more they avoid, the more you accommodate.

- Second (boxes 1, 5, and 6), the vicious cycle of recovery avoidance and minimization. Recovery avoidance (box 1) leads the family to minimize (box 5), which increases anxiety and anger in the recovery avoider (box 6), which in turn leads to defensiveness and more recovery avoidance (box 1). The more you minimize, the more your loved one avoids recovery, and the more they avoid, the more you minimize.

- Finally (boxes 2, 4, and 5), how accommodating makes the family more likely to minimize. Accommodation (box 2) produces additional burdens for the family (box 4), which increases their emotional distress and thus their propensity to minimize (box 5). The more you accommodate, the more likely you are to minimize, and both perpetuate recovery avoidance.

To better understand how the family trap develops, let's examine one family's story in greater detail. You may remember Sara from the Introduction. She's married to Gabriel, who's been struggling with depression. Sara and her daughter, Ana, have been trying to help Gabriel. The diagram shows the Garcias' family trap.

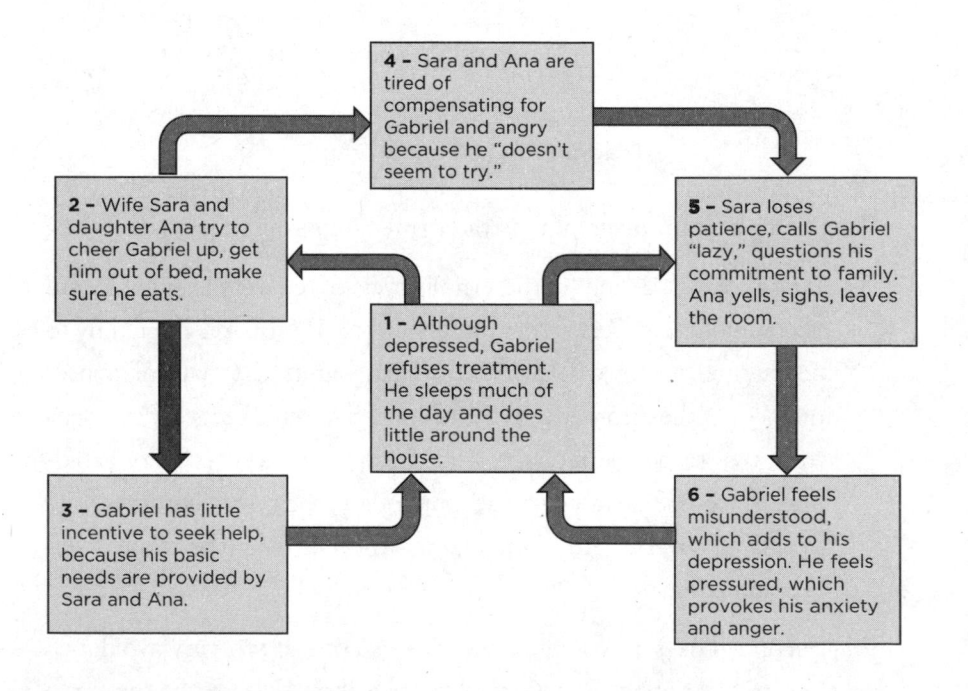

DIAGRAM 2: The Garcia's Family Trap

The Garcias are stuck. The more Sara and Ana accommodate, the more Gabriel relies on them and the less incentive he has to seek help. Although the family accommodations help Gabriel get by in the short run, over time the burden takes a toll on Sara and Ana. They're becoming increasingly resentful and unable to keep their cool. More and more, they find themselves criticizing and nagging Gabriel or giving him the cold shoulder. The burden of being stuck in a family trap can be overwhelming, and Sara and Ana are only human. But so is Gabriel. He feels they don't understand what he's up against. And the continued pressure for him to change only makes Gabriel feel more anxious and inadequate, which makes the prospect of seeking recovery seem even more remote.

Gabriel, Sara, and Ana are all victims of recovery avoidance. They're captured in a trap and don't know how to get out. Of course, Sara and Ana know they could just stop accommodating, but they're afraid of what will happen if they do. They're not proud that they minimize, and they know it isn't working, but it feels as if they'd be giving up if they stopped pressuring Gabriel to seek help. And giving up's the last thing they want to do.

If you're in the family trap, you may be facing some of the same dilemmas as the Garcia family. When you're trapped, it's easy to feel hopeless, to think there's no way out. But take heart. There *is* a way out, and you're about to learn it.

Moving Forward

You now know how you've contributed to recovery avoidance, and how accommodating and minimizing make things worse. You realize that the more you accommodate and minimize, the more your loved one avoids. We hope you also understand there's no benefit in second guessing or judging yourself for how you've responded to recovery avoidance in the past. You couldn't possibly have known how to deal with it before it happened to your family. But things are different now. You know what not to do and why, and you'll soon learn what to do instead and how to go about it. Let's move on to chapter 3.

The Way Out: Pursuing Family Well-Being

Main Point: In this chapter, you'll learn a very different, more effective approach to recovery avoidance: the pursuit of family well-being. You'll learn why this approach can work for your family and why it's your best chance to escape the family trap.

You've probably figured out by now that, in order to escape the family trap, eventually you'll have to reduce accommodating and minimizing. But to do this successfully you'll need to know what to do instead and how to go about it. Spoiler alert: We're going to ask you to change how you view the problem. To help us get started, consider the iconic serenity prayer:

> ...Grant me the serenity to accept the things I cannot change, courage to change the things I can, and the wisdom to know the difference...

When you're in the family trap, you must come to accept something very important—and a little tough: your inability to change your loved one. Sometimes people do influence others to change, but, short of brute force, that happens only when the person you're trying to influence is receptive and free from opposing forces. A loved one who's avoiding recovery is neither receptive nor free. When you accommodate or minimize someone who's avoiding recovery, your efforts are focused on changing someone else, someone who has strong reasons not to change. And your success depends on that someone else changing, which means your fate—your happiness and satisfaction, your sense of security and comfort in knowledge of their safety and health—rests on something that's simply not in your control.

You may also struggle to change the things you can control—your own behavior. You make attempts, like Sara and Ana did—trying to set boundaries or pulling back on accommodations—but then you don't follow through, or you find yourself collapsing into minimizing behavior, like criticizing or guilt-tripping your loved one. It's not that you lack courage or self-control. You've been inadequately prepared for the resistance you've encountered. Attempting to change your behavior before being fully prepared for your loved one's reaction leaves you vulnerable to fear, hesitancy, and, ultimately, retreat. And nothing changes.

Rethinking How You Approach Recovery Avoidance

Escaping the family trap requires that you focus on what you can change, what's in your control—chiefly, your own behavior. If you want to escape the trap successfully, you must stop waiting for your loved one to change. Instead, you'll change your behavior by reducing how much you accommodate and minimize. We're not saying to give up on your loved one—quite the opposite. Dedicating your efforts to things in your control is the best hope for a better life for you both. Easier said than done, but we'll guide you through the process.

As your priorities shift to what you can control, you'll be freer to focus on improving your own well-being and that of any family member or friend who's willing to join you. That's why it's called the family well-being approach. It prioritizes the welfare of the entire family, including you. So initially your efforts will focus on reducing the negative impact of recovery avoidance on *your* life.

There are two very good reasons to focus on yourself. The first, you already know—because your behavior is something you can actually change. But the second is very important: It enables you to stop contributing to the family trap. The fewer accommodations you make, especially those that interfere with your life, the greater your well-being. And the greater your well-being, the less minimizing you'll do and the better equipped you'll be to deal effectively with your loved one. When your well-being is compromised, so is your ability to constructively assist others. (Think of flight attendants telling you to secure your own oxygen mask before assisting children and others who need help.)

The Path to Family Well-Being

Let's reexamine how the family trap operates. As you take another look at what happens to families, note that in the "Perpetuating Recovery Avoidance" diagram we've highlighted boxes 2 and 5—the moments when you accommodate your loved one's recovery avoidance or respond to them by minimizing. These are the actions you'll eventually want to reduce—the two components of the trap in your direct control. Changing these responses is your way out.

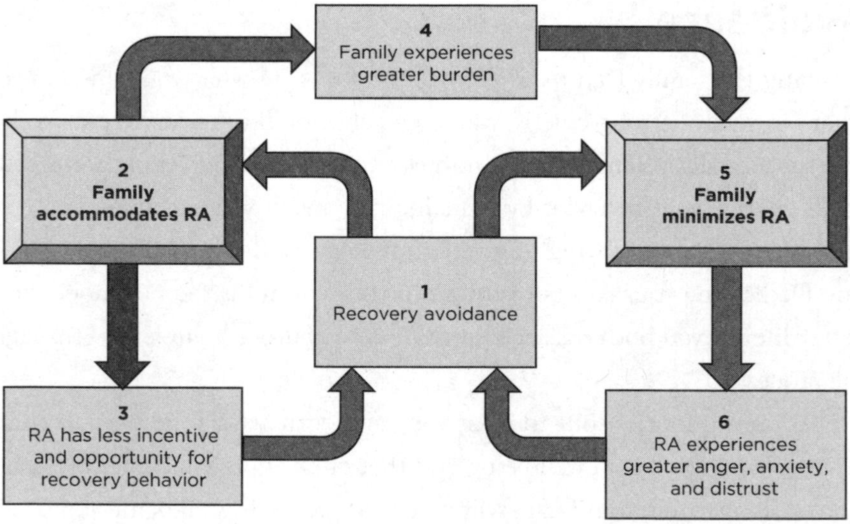

Diagram 3: The Family Trap: Perpetuating Recovery Avoidance

Before discussing what happens when you begin to escape the family trap, there's one more term to know: *recovery behavior*. This includes any act consistent with the pursuit of improved health or functioning or the resolution of problems.

It's the opposite of recovery avoidance. Recovery behavior of course includes seeking treatment. However, any move away from impairment and toward recovery, big or small, is considered recovery behavior. Examples include even modest improvements in functioning, like taking on a new chore or improving self-care, or reductions in dysfunctional behavior, like fewer negative statements or less-frequent temper outbursts. Recovery behavior also includes the pursuit of resources (a self-help book, support group, advice from a friend, and so on) that might potentially contribute to recovery. Recovery behavior is what emerges when recovery avoidance begins to fade. It gives you something, however minor, to encourage and reward in your loved one. Change doesn't always need to be big or final to count as progress. Keep this in mind, so you don't miss opportunities to recognize when things are moving in the right direction.

Now consider what happens when you reduce accommodating and minimizing. Once again, in the diagram "Reversing Recovery Avoidance," we've highlighted boxes 2 and 5 to emphasize the part of the trap that's in your control, only this time we're noting what you need to do differently.

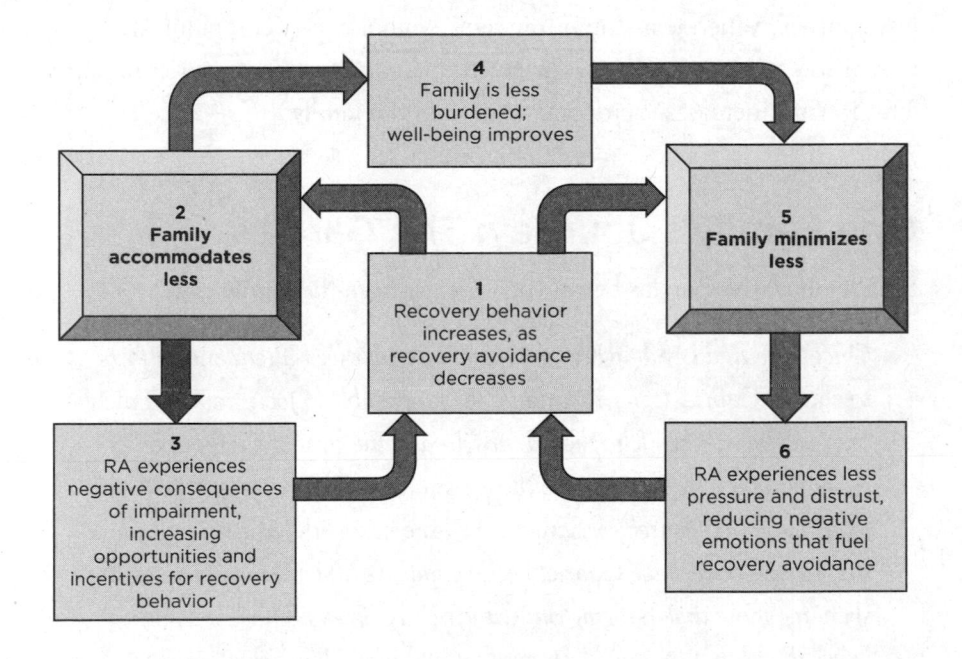

Diagram 4: Escaping the Family Trap: Reversing Recovery Avoidance

First, look at boxes 1, 2, and 3. When accommodation decreases, recovery avoiders begin to experience the consequences of their disorder. Why is that so important? Because consequences incentivize people to seek recovery. You can't force your loved one to pursue recovery, but you can stop doing things that make it easier to avoid recovery.

Another very important thing happens when you stop accommodating: Your life eventually improves. Look at boxes 2, 4, and 5. Less accommodating leads to less family burden and improved well-being, which leads to less minimizing. This is not surprising. When you're spending less time accommodating, you feel better. And when you feel better, you act better. That means you're less likely to respond to your loved one by minimizing.

Now look at boxes 1, 5, and 6. See what happens when the family stops minimizing. First of all, the person who's been avoiding recovery becomes less angry and defensive, because the family is no longer pressing for change. The critical tone, the lecturing, the pleading have stopped. There are fewer family arguments, and the overall family environment has improved. For now, the family has given up trying to make their loved one change, so there's less conflict. When you stop minimizing, you also stop communicating the unrealistic expectation that your loved one can change at your command. This in turn increases their comfort around the family.

One Family's Journey: The Garcias

Let's see how the Garcias began their escape from the family trap.

Once Sara and her daughter accepted that their well-intentioned efforts to change Gabriel weren't working, they were able to focus more on their own behavior. They felt relieved, absolved of the constant responsibility to get him to do things; this made them less angry. They were also able to focus more on themselves. Sara realized she missed the artistic endeavors she'd abandoned since Gabriel became impaired. Her daughter started spending more time hanging out with friends. They both were doing fewer things that generated resentment and more things that enriched their lives. By changing their behavior, Sara and her daughter changed the family dynamics. And Gabriel responded in turn. He gradually became more self-reliant and spent less time defending his self-defeating behavior. He also began taking greater initiative in the family, and of his own accord—not because Sara or Ana had compelled him in ways that he'd usually resent.

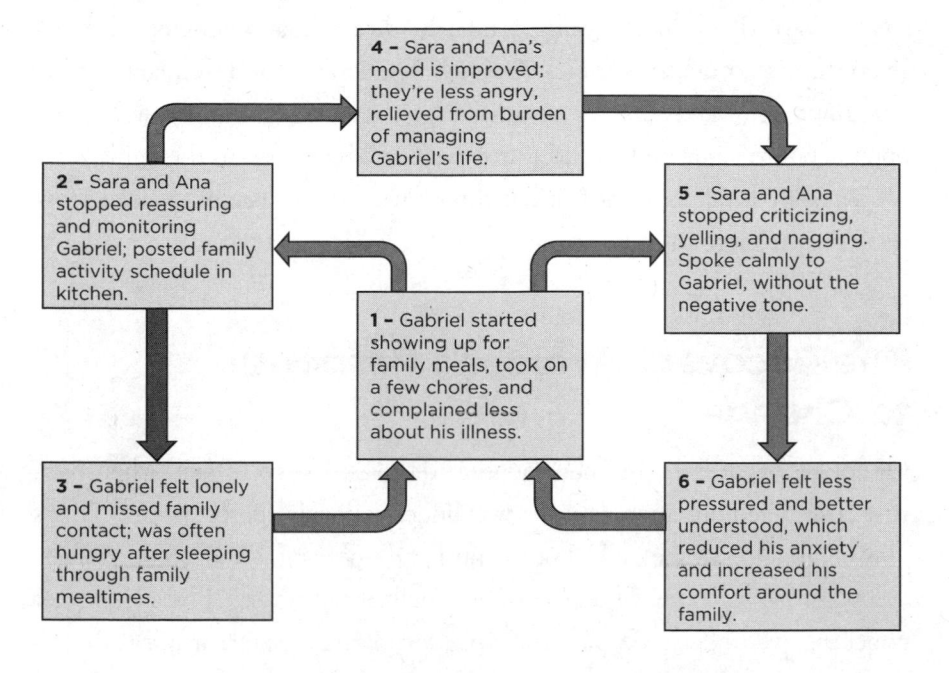

Diagram 5: Escaping the Garcias' Family Trap

The Garcias' story illustrates how healthy family change realistically occurs—in steps, gradually over time. As Sara and her daughter changed their behavior, they also changed the conditions under which Gabriel was living. Those conditions gradually shifted the family momentum away from recovery avoidance and toward recovery behavior; away from behavior that generates conflict with the recovery avoider and toward behavior that promotes family well-being; away from behavior that fosters dependency in the recovery avoider and toward behavior that advances self-sufficiency. Though things in the Garcia household were far from perfect, they were clearly heading in the right direction.

At this point, you could rightfully point out Gabriel still hasn't returned to work or sought treatment. *After all,* you might think, *isn't that the goal?* Actually, no, it isn't, at least not at first. Certainly, Sara and her daughter hope someday to get back the Gabriel they once knew. But they've come to understand that change happens in steps, and they've learned to appreciate the strides Gabriel has made so far. They know the steps he makes now can establish a foundation for future change. They also remember how bad things were when their efforts were primarily directed at changing Gabriel. Everything's no longer all about Gabriel. The family's overall quality of life has improved, and that's the initial priority of the family well-being approach—to value and attend to the welfare of everyone in the family.

Keep in mind, Sara and her daughter have only just begun to make progress. There's more to come.

The Recovery Avoider's Response to Change

Of course, what Sara and her daughter did wasn't easy. In fact, when Sara first considered our approach, she was understandably apprehensive. "That's all well and good," she said, "but my husband's not going to like the changes you want me to make. Things could get ugly at our house." If you share her concerns, we understand. It's true, your loved one probably will feel threatened by some of the changes you make. You're withdrawing support they feel is necessary to cope. And that will naturally generate resistance, at least initially.

When a loved one with recovery avoidance resists change, families usually respond by retreating. Begrudgingly, they resume their accommodations and fall back into the family trap. Sara and her daughter had been particularly immobilized by their fear that Gabriel might commit suicide. Each time they'd try to implement change, Gabriel would say he didn't want to live and wonder out loud if they'd be better off without him. Out of fear, Sara and her daughter would resume their accommodations, including the pep talks and reassurance. And once again, they were back in the trap.

It's understandable why families respond the way they do. They often feel there's no other choice. And certain possibilities—like harm coming to a loved one—feel so terrifying you can become unwilling to follow through with the changes you had planned. But retreat is not the only alternative, as Sara and Ana learned. We prepared them for the various ways Gabriel might resist their efforts to change. We anticipated his resistance, developed plans for how to respond, and practiced those responses ahead of time. If Gabriel said anything that made them feel uneasy about his safety, for instance, Sara and Ana planned to take it seriously. They would immediately call an ambulance to take Gabriel to the emergency room—no exceptions.

They also told Gabriel the plan ahead of time. This time around their presentation was not laced with minimizing and accommodating. They spoke with compassion and respect, they told Gabriel they loved him, but they didn't participate in a prolonged effort to cheer him up, provide reassurance, or convince him to agree. They simply stated what they were going to do in response to a clearly identified behavior. And, importantly, they did what they said they'd do. It wasn't always easy, but clarifying the plan ahead of time and following through taught Gabriel that his actions would be taken seriously. And the comparatively swift, calm manner in which Sara and Ana followed their plan meant there was little accommodating and minimizing that might reinforce future incidences of his behavior.

Reductions in accommodating and minimizing are generally followed by improvements in the family environment, but you do have to get past your loved one's initial resistance. In the short run, you'll likely encounter pushback from them and an increase in family tension. But if you're properly prepared beforehand and you follow through with your plan, the tension and resistance diminish quicker than you might think. We'll explain this more in step 2 of the program, when you'll be redefining the problem and setting goals. But for now, keep two things in mind. First, you're not going to stop all accommodations at once. You'll phase accommodations out over time, which is less stressful for everyone, which in turn means less resistance. Second, you'll be reducing minimizing behavior at the same time you're reducing accommodations. And you'll make a commitment to do so when you present your plan. The promise of less minimizing is usually well received by someone in recovery avoidance, which helps temper resistance to the accommodations you're about to withdraw.

Your Loved One's Future

It's natural for families to worry about their loved one's future. Even when they understand the initial focus of the approach is on themselves, they can't help hoping the changes they make will create the climate and motivation necessary to spur their loved one to participate effectively in treatment. Indeed, this sometimes happens. But what's more likely, especially early on, is the gradual emergence of smaller behavior changes compatible with recovery. You'll recall that when we checked in with the Garcias shortly after they'd begun implementing the family well-being approach, Gabriel had not yet sought treatment. But he was starting to do more around the house without being prompted—behavior that had been nonexistent when there was more accommodating and minimizing going on.

It may be disappointing to learn that your initial efforts might not immediately eliminate your loved one's ambivalence about treatment. But keep in mind three important points. First, when you reduce accommodations and stop minimizing, there's almost always some movement toward recovery. This means you've begun to reverse the trajectory of recovery avoidance. Research has demonstrated families can make meaningful reductions in accommodations (VanDyke, Pollard, Harper, and Conlon 2015) that can lead to significant improvements in an impaired individual's condition (Lebowitz et al. 2020), even when that individual has had no contact with a therapist. Second, just because major changes don't occur right away doesn't mean they won't happen eventually. The processes that drive recovery avoidance can't be turned around overnight, and some loved ones naturally take longer than others to respond to the changes their families implement. Third, the initial objective of escaping the family trap is not to change your loved one; it's to improve the well-being of the family, something every family can achieve to some degree.

It can be hard to accept the idea of putting the family's well-being *before* the task of changing your loved one and getting them to recovery. Take a moment to process that now, perhaps writing some thoughts in a journal. What does that bring to mind for you? Does the idea of letting go of what you've been doing feel scary? And are you beginning to see how focusing on what's firmly within your control—how you behave with your loved one— might be helpful for you and your family too?

Above all, keep in mind that down the road, once your family's well-being has improved, you'll be able to do things you couldn't have done before. With greater emotional health and a better relationship with your loved one, you'll be able to implement a strategic approach to promote their recovery behavior. And you'll be better equipped to do so successfully. In fact, the final step of our approach is to create a family environment that fosters recovery. But all of this must wait until you've taken sufficient care of yourself.

The Five Steps of the Family Well-Being Approach

As we discussed in the Introduction, the family well-being approach involves five steps. The chapters ahead will guide you through each step as you pursue greater family well-being.

Step 1: Prepare for crises. In this step, you'll anticipate potential crises and develop a plan to keep them from jeopardizing your success. If you're ill-prepared for crises, you're less likely to make the kind of changes you need to improve family well-being.

Step 2: Redefine the problem. In this step, you'll identify the ways in which your loved one's behavior has negatively impacted your life and decide what changes you'll make. Those changes might include recapturing activities you value, reducing the burden of accommodating, and decreasing family conflict and distress.

Step 3: Embrace valued activity. In this step, you'll develop and implement a plan to reintroduce valued activities into your life. We'll help you problem solve any obstacles that arise and show you how to modify your plan when they do. Embracing valued activity is an important part of enhancing your well-being.

Step 4: Ease family distress. In this step, you'll work on reducing counterproductive interactions with your loved one and adopting more constructive behavior. You'll learn how to reduce your accommodations and scale back minimizing.

Step 5. Create a recovery-friendly environment. When you're ready, in this step, you'll learn how to encourage recovery behavior in your loved one without the power struggles of the past. Instead of pressuring them to change, you'll be creating incentives that promote behavior compatible with recovery.

Moving Forward

You now know a new way to approach recovery avoidance. You know that escaping the family trap—the cycle of unproductive accommodation and minimization on your part, continued recovery avoidance on the part of your loved one, and the entrenched power struggle between you—starts with changing your behavior. When you stop accommodating, you create greater incentive for change and more opportunities for them to practice recovery behavior. And when you stop minimizing, you reduce negative emotions that fuel recovery avoidance, and you create a family environment that's more compatible with positive behavior change. Most importantly, all of this improves your well-being. You'll be better prepared, both emotionally and strategically, to influence your loved one to move toward recovery, including pursuing and effectively participating in treatment.

It's almost time to start the process, but there's one more thing to learn. You're more likely to be successful if you know the obstacles you may encounter and how to deal with them. That's up next in chapter 4.

CHAPTER 4

Potential Threats to Your Success

Main Point: You'll learn the common obstacles that can jeopardize your pursuit of family well-being, and how to overcome them so you can successfully complete the steps outlined in this book.

Let's be frank: the pursuit of family well-being is not without its challenges. Several potential obstacles can hinder your efforts to escape the family trap. We say this not to discourage you, but to increase your chances for success. The more you know about potential obstacles, the better you'll be able to deal with them if and when they arise.

Although obstacles can come from many directions, they usually emerge within the family. You may already know this if you've tried to make changes before. Perhaps your loved one has pushed back, or another family member undermined your efforts. When it comes to escaping the family trap, anyone in the family can become an obstacle—even you.

Obstacles Your Loved One Might Present

The most common reason families remain trapped is concern about their loved one's resistance. And it's a valid concern. Recovery avoiders almost always protest when family members try to stop accommodating. The resistance may amount to little more than mild protest, but it can also escalate rapidly, posing a serious threat to the family's safety or welfare. Loved ones in the throes of recovery avoidance may threaten suicide, damage property, or become physically aggressive when families try to implement change. Given the stakes, it's easy to see why families fall back into old patterns of accommodating and minimizing. It feels too risky to do otherwise.

When faced with a situation like this, you're in an incredibly difficult bind. If you try making changes, you risk having to contend with a crisis. If you don't change, you remain stuck in the trap and risk having to deal with future crises. Neither option is tenable. Fortunately, there's a third option— to change your behavior, but only after being adequately prepared for the potential consequences. That means: (1) having a sound plan for protecting the family's safety; (2) being prepared and willing to follow through with the plan; and (3) telling your loved one about the plan ahead of time, so they're clear about the consequences of certain behaviors. We'll do all of that in step 1.

Obstacles Other Family Members Might Present

Other family members could also resist the changes you want to make. If others aren't ready to escape the trap, they can easily interfere with your efforts and blunt the effects of your desired changes. Take the Garcia family, for example. If Sara stopped accommodating and minimizing, but Ana continued to monitor Gabriel, give him pep talks, and criticize him, Gabriel's behavior might not have changed, at least not to the extent it did. Sara and Ana's unified approach was more effective.

You've gotten this far in the book, so chances are good you're ready to escape. But what about others in the family? Who else is ready to escape with you? It's important to clarify this from the start. Meet with your family to discuss the issue. Educate them about what you've been reading, and encourage them to read this book as well. If they're on board, great! You can coordinate your efforts and work together to implement the steps outlined in this book.

If they're not on board, all is not lost. Escaping the trap may be easier when the family's united, but it's possible to escape on your own—to improve the quality of your life, even if no one else joins in. We've seen it happen many times. And even if it's ultimately only you who makes the change, well, that's one less family member in the trap. Also keep in mind, changes in one person can create a ripple effect throughout the family. You may be the first to escape, but perhaps not the last. As you change, others in the family have to adapt to your changes, and that sometimes creates incentive for others in the family to change their behavior as well. Just think, if Sara had changed and Ana hadn't, the sole burden of accommodating Gabriel would have fallen squarely on Ana. And that additional burden could have eventually influenced Ana to join Sara in her journey out of the trap.

Obstacles You Might Present

It may sound odd to consider yourself an obstacle, but like all of us, you too are vulnerable to recovery avoidance. Your own personal issues could interfere with your ability to pursue family well-being. We want you to be prepared for all the possible obstacles, even if one of them is you.

Recall the different factors that drive recovery avoidance—recovery-interfering beliefs, skill deficits, motivation deficits, and incentive deficits. (For a reminder, revisit chapter 1.) Your effort to read this book probably means you have sufficient motivation, but that still leaves three potential sources of recovery avoidance. Two of them—skill deficits and incentive deficits—will be addressed later in this book. If you follow the steps of the family well-being approach, you'll learn the skills you need and how to keep disincentives from derailing you.

That leaves one potential source of recovery avoidance—recovery-interfering beliefs. Not the beliefs you learned about in chapter 1—your loved one's recovery-interfering beliefs, like "I don't have a problem" or "Treatment won't work." In this chapter, we're talking about *your* beliefs—the ones that can prevent you from pursuing well-being and can make you too afraid, guilt-ridden, or angry to follow through with your escape from the family trap. In particular, misguided beliefs about personal responsibility, family obligation, fairness, and emotions can easily lead you astray.

We've identified eight recovery-interfering beliefs common in families dealing with a loved one with recovery avoidance. We call these beliefs *myths* because they're based on faulty assumptions that justify accommodating and minimizing and lead families away from well-being. We'll describe each myth, the fallacy behind it, and a healthy alternative belief that promotes well-being. Please read this next section carefully to see if any of these beliefs apply to you.

Myth 1: "The only way for my life to improve is if my loved one gets better."

The fallacy: This myth recognizes only one way your life can improve and rests your well-being completely on the behavior of another person. It'll almost certainly be better for you if your loved one recovers, but that's not in your control. What if they choose not to seek help, seek help but don't participate adequately, or don't respond to treatment? These possibilities may be difficult to accept. But once you do, you can refocus your efforts on improving the quality of your life. That's important whether your loved one gets better or not.

The healthy alternative: "It would be nice if my loved one got better, but my family's well-being is too important to wait for that to happen."

Myth 2: "It's selfish to focus on my own well-being."

The fallacy: This myth portrays healthy concern about yourself as something shameful. The word "selfish" is a put-down, not an accurate or useful description of taking care of oneself. It implies that concern about your own well-being is inconsiderate, that it's somehow harmful to someone else. On the contrary, taking care of yourself usually helps others (see myth #3 for more on this).

The healthy alternative: "Focusing on my well-being is in the family's best interests and allows me to provide a healthy model for others."

Myth 3: "Pursuing my own well-being will jeopardize my efforts to help my loved one."

The fallacy: This myth incorrectly suggests that helping yourself will make you less able to help your loved one. The truth is quite the opposite. When you're less burdened by frustration, guilt, and other negative emotions, you'll actually be more effective in dealing with other people, including your loved one. Can you honestly say that your interactions with them in your current state of mind are always level-headed and constructive?

The healthy alternative: "Improving my well-being will make me better equipped to deal with my loved one."

Myth 4: "My loved one will be upset if I pursue my own well-being."

The fallacy: The prediction that your loved one will get upset isn't wrong; that certainly might happen. In fact, you should be fully prepared for this and plan how you'll handle it. The fallacy is in the myth's underlying assumptions: (1) that you can control whether they get upset, and (2) that they won't get upset if you stay the same. You really don't have much control over whether they get upset. You *can* choose whether or not you do something helpful for yourself and the family.

The healthy alternative: "I have control over whether I pursue well-being, not whether my loved one gets upset."

Myth 5: "Being upset will harm my loved one."

The fallacy: This myth wrongly assigns danger to normal human experiences. In fact, we're designed to feel an entire range of emotions, including unpleasant ones. Some people don't handle emotions as well as others, but that doesn't mean the emotion itself is directly harming them.

The healthy alternative: "Being upset is unpleasant, but it doesn't harm my loved one."

Myth 6: "It's my responsibility to protect my loved one from negative feelings."

The fallacy: This myth inappropriately gives you responsibility for someone else's feelings. If you'd like to avoid making someone feel bad for no good reason, that's fair. But you have a very good reason to risk making a recovery avoider feel uncomfortable. You're trying to improve the family's well-being. It's not your responsibility to protect your loved one from feeling bad at the expense of other family members.

The healthy alternative: "Pursuing my well-being and the family's well-being is my responsibility, not how others feel about it."

Myth 7: "I shouldn't have to be the one to change."

The fallacy: This myth is based on the fantasy of a world that doesn't exist, a world in which things are always fair. People usually use the word "should" when they don't want to deal with the world as it is; that is, "should" refers to how you feel things ought to be. But it has little to do with the world in which you live, the world about which you must make real decisions. In the real world, changing your behavior is what you have the most control over and what you're most likely to succeed at.

The healthy alternative: "I'll change when doing so is within my control and in my best interests."

Myth 8: "I should be able to cope without getting help for myself."

The fallacy: There's that "should" word again. This myth refers to a world in which people are all-knowing and never need assistance from others—not a world any of us exists in. In reality, reasonable people seek assistance from those who have expertise or access to resources they don't have. Knowing when to seek help is not a weakness. It's a strength that improves your ability to function. Don't be the person who gets lost because you're too proud to ask for directions.

The healthy alternative: "I intend to use any resource that could help maximize my chances for success."

Which of these myths have influenced your behavior? Do the fallacies we've identified and the alternatives we provide help loosen the myths' grip on you? If you like, take some time to write about this, before you move on.

Moving Forward

You now know the obstacles you could face as you attempt to escape the family trap. You've learned that those obstacles can emerge from anyone in the family, including you—and you've learned that you have the power, with sufficient awareness and foresight, to steer clear of them. You've learned a lot so far. Now it's time to begin your escape. On to part 2 of the book, where you'll begin implementing the family well-being approach.

PART 2

Escaping the Family Trap: What You Need to Do

In this part of the book, we'll explain the family well-being approach and how you can apply it to your family. But before you start step 1, it's important to let your loved one know about what's happening.

Telling Your Loved One About Your Planned Changes

You're about to make some pretty important changes in your behavior—changes that could dramatically improve your family's well-being. To facilitate the changes you hope to make, you'll need to communicate effectively. That's why, each step of the way, we'll be encouraging you to keep your loved one informed. When it's time, you'll tell them how you plan to handle crises differently (step 1), how you plan to embrace valued activity (step 3), how you plan to cut back on accommodating and minimizing (step 4), and how you plan to incentivize them to move toward recovery (step 5).

At each step, we'll recommend a similar method of communication. We'll ask that you:

1. Write out a plan that details the changes you're going to make and when they'll start.

2. Write a letter to your loved one, introducing the reasons you're making the changes and what you hope will come of it.

3. Meet with them to give them the letter, with your plan attached, and to answer any questions they might have.

Guidelines follow for each of these efforts. We'll be referring you back to these guidelines each time you're about to communicate a plan to your loved one.

Writing Out the Changes You Plan to Make

When implementing any change that affects your loved one, it's important they know exactly what you plan to do and when you plan to do it. For each type of change—each step you take toward family well-being—we'll provide you with a form to help you organize your thoughts and write out your plan. These plans aren't meant just to inform your loved one. They're for you as well, to help keep you on track. The chapters ahead will show you how each form can be used to organize your plan.

Writing a Letter to Your Loved One

Your first instinct may be to speak with your loved one, rather than use a letter to communicate. We understand that talking might feel more natural to you. However, please consider the advantages of a letter. Putting things in writing allows you to gather your thoughts and refine how you present the plan. Most notably, it allows you to edit out any minimizing statements that might slip into your initial attempt to express yourself. Finally, putting things in writing documents the information you want to share and therefore reduces the chances of subsequent disputes about what your loved one was or wasn't told. It also saves you from having to reclarify details of the plan repeatedly. You can simply remind them, "It's all in the letter." That's important, because subsequent conversations about what you're doing or why you're doing it place you at risk of slipping into minimizing.

Each time you plan to implement changes, you can introduce your plan in a letter. For each step, we provide sample letters you can use as models. Everyone involved in the plan should have a copy of each letter and the plan.

Here are a few tips to consider when writing your letters:

- **Be positive.** Express your hopes for the family's future.

- **Take responsibility for your behavior.** Acknowledge that you've made mistakes and would like to do better. This doesn't mean it's all your fault. It means you're able to admit your contribution to the problem—something you hope your loved one will be able to do as well someday.

- **Focus on what you're going to do differently,** not what your loved one should or shouldn't do. They will decide how to respond to the changes you make.

- **State positive reasons why you're making the changes you've planned.** For example: "to improve our family's well-being," "to improve how I take care of myself," or "to improve how I treat you."

- **Provide a specific start date for the plan.** Unless the situation is urgent, you'll want to give your loved one at least one week's notice. That allows time for them to get used to the idea.

Meeting with Your Loved One

Once you've mapped your plan out and written your letter, schedule a meeting with your loved one to present your plan. Try to set a time when things are the least hectic and everyone involved is most likely to be available. If meeting in person is not possible, a virtual or telephone meeting will do. Provide them with a written copy of the letter and the plan you're about to implement. Allow them sufficient time to read and absorb the material. If you think it would be helpful, let them have the material a day or more in advance of your meeting.

Be careful not to speak too much while your loved one's looking over the letter and your plan. Allow the material you've presented to express your thoughts. Invite questions, but answer only questions you feel are sincere attempts to understand the changes you're planning; for example, questions that might help clarify certain details of the plan. But be careful. Things can go wrong quickly. Beware of unproductive questioning. Don't answer questions that've already been answered. Instead, point out where the answer can be found in the materials you've provided. Avoid responding to questions that communicate resistance, like "Why are you doing this?". You've already provided the answer in your letter, so this kind of question isn't really an attempt to understand the plan better. Finally, don't respond to questions that are off topic ("When can I get my own place?"). Stay focused on the current plan and end the meeting as soon as there are no more useful questions. Some additional tips:

- **Remain calm.** Try to maintain a respectful tone, even if your loved one becomes provocative. Consider pausing the meeting if you feel yourself slipping into minimizing; resume the meeting when you're less upset.

- **Expect some pushback.** This is natural. Your loved one may see the changes you're making as a threat.

- **Allow your loved one to be upset.** Empathize ("We realize this may be difficult for you"), but don't try to make them feel better or convince them these changes are a good thing. That puts you at too much risk of falling into minimizing or accommodating.

- **Avoid arguments.** You're not there to convince them of anything, just to tell them what's going to happen. If they remain argumentative, simply end the meeting and walk away.

- **Don't negotiate.** That will almost certainly lead to minimizing. They need to know what you're planning to do, but their approval is not required.

- **Don't worry if your loved one refuses to read the letter.** If you try to force this, it could easily turn into a power struggle. Your job is to present the letter, not to make them read it. You'll be implementing your plan whether they read it or not. Experiencing the consequences of the changes you make, especially if they're unexpected, allows them to learn the value of reading any future plans you present.

- **Role-play ahead of time if needed.** If you're nervous about how you'll handle the meeting, practice it with another family member before meeting with your loved one. You may feel this is unnecessary, but it's better to be overprepared than to be caught by surprise. Remember the old joke? Question: "Hey, mister, how do I get to Carnegie Hall?" Answer: "Practice, practice, practice!"

Introducing Your Loved One to Your Pursuit of Family Well-Being

Now it's time to write your very first letter. Unlike the letters you'll write later, this letter won't include a detailed plan describing specific changes you're going to make. You don't have a plan like that anyway, not yet. This letter is to foreshadow the coming changes—to announce the journey you're about to begin. You'll declare your intent to improve the emotional well-being of the family; you'll acknowledge that you need to change your behavior. This sets the tone for all the specific changes you'll be making in the months ahead. You may also want to mention the help you've received to support your effort—for example, this book, a therapist, a support group, or any other resource you're using. Getting help is a powerful statement about your commitment. It demonstrates how important improving your family's well-being is to you.

Here's an example that illustrates how you might introduce the pursuit of family well-being to your loved one. Consistent with the approach we recommend, this letter emphasizes the changes *you'll* be making, not how *they* need to change. We encourage you to maintain this message throughout your attempt to escape the family trap.

Dear _____,

We want to improve the quality of our relationship with you and create a better family environment for all of us. We understand that the way we interact with you has not always been helpful. We realize we have been too focused on changing you and not focused enough on changing ourselves. For that, we apologize.

In the months ahead, we'll be making changes to improve things a little bit at a time. We'll share our goals and what we're up to as we go along. If there is a particular change we plan to make that might affect you, we'll try to tell you ahead of time. We ask for your patience and understanding as we attempt to improve our family's well-being.

Love,

_____

Now write a letter to your loved one, based on the model we've provided. Try not to be too wordy. Keep it short and sweet. Give your loved one the letter and get ready to begin step 1. That's where you'll prepare for the kinds of crises that can occur as you implement change.

Prepare for Crises

There is no harm in hoping for the best, as long as you are prepared for the worst.

—Stephen King

CHAPTER 5

Developing Your Family Crisis Plan

Main Point: In this chapter, we'll describe the kinds of crises that can happen in families dealing with recovery avoidance and how to keep them from derailing your pursuit of family well-being.

Perhaps you're wondering why a crisis plan is the first step to family well-being. The answer is straightforward—it'll be harder to succeed if you don't have one ready if and when you need it. When you're unprepared, you're more likely to react impulsively, which means you're likely to rely on accommodating and minimizing, and that keeps you and your loved one stuck. We recognize that crises are scary, especially if you don't know what to do. Step 1 will help you develop a plan designed to ensure your family's safety while limiting accommodating and minimizing as much as possible.

Let's Get Started

We define a crisis as any situation involving threatened or actual injury or death to a person or destruction or loss of valued personal property.

Not every stressful situation is a crisis. To qualify as a crisis, a situation must involve potential harm that is both serious and imminent. A *crisis behavior* is any behavior that creates a crisis, and every potential crisis requires a family crisis plan.

We'll show you three different family crisis plans. You'll see a plan for suicidal behavior, one for violence, and another for property theft or damage.

These are the most common crisis behaviors encountered by families dealing with recovery avoidance. Notice that each plan describes the type of crisis being targeted, the ultimate goal of the plan, and the action steps the family will take to achieve that goal. And each plan includes decisive action to ensure the family's safety with little or no accommodating or minimizing. This is important because research has shown us that how people respond to crisis behavior affects the likelihood of future crisis behavior (DeCou, Comtois, and Landes 2019; Linehan et al. 1993).

Suicidal Behavior

Suicidal behavior includes talking about, hinting at, threatening, or attempting suicide. Families dealing with suicidal behavior often get stuck trying to determine whether their loved one "really means it," or trying to talk them out of feeling bad. These are understandable responses, especially given the stakes, but they can do more harm than good in the long run. Take a look, for instance, at how the Garcia family dealt with suicidal behavior before their family crisis plan was developed:

> *When Gabriel felt down, he'd wonder out loud if his wife and daughter would be better off without him. At first, Sara and Ana would try to cheer Gabriel up. Then Sara would plead with him to snap out of it. Ana would often let out an exasperated sigh and head to her room in a huff. Sometimes they'd both challenge Gabriel, detailing all the reasons why his life was "not that bad."*

Sara and Ana were spending too much time accommodating and minimizing instead of taking decisive action to ensure Gabriel's safety. They needed a crisis plan to change how they'd respond to Gabriel's suicidal talk. Once the plan was developed, Sara and Ana told Gabriel about it. Here's what they came up with:

Family Crisis Plan: Suicidal Behavior

The Crisis	Our Goal	Action Steps
You say or do something we feel suggests you're thinking about harming yourself.	To protect you from harm.	We'll take the risk seriously. We'll ask: "Are you able to keep yourself safe?" If your answer is anything other than "Yes," we'll contact Behavioral Health Response by calling 314-469-6644 (or 988). We'll request they take whatever steps are necessary to ensure you're safe from harm.

We realize the decision to use an emergency service can be complicated. The quality of available resources varies greatly between communities. Sara and Ana were fortunate. Their community had a local organization that specifically assists with mental health emergencies. If you don't have this kind of organization in your community, you might call 988—the Suicide and Crisis Lifeline—or 911 if that service functions effectively where you live. If your loved one is in treatment, we encourage you to contact their provider. Many mental health clinicians take emergency calls twenty-four hours a day. For a list of additional resources, consult our online resources page: http://www.newharbinger.com/53134.

Violence

Violence includes threatening, attempting, or actually harming someone. Families dealing with violent behavior often get into power struggles with their loved one or spend too much time trying to talk them down. The Robinson family struggled with this.

Steve and Stacy Robinson's son, Robert, had severe germ fears and frequent outbursts when his family didn't follow his "decontamination" instructions. On one occasion, he picked up a knife and stated that his sister Olivia "would pay" for not following the rules. When Steve learned about the incident, he responded by calling Robert names and threatening to "throw him out on the street" if he ever did that again. Stacy defended Robert and assured the others that he'd never hurt anyone in the family.

Stacy and Steve were working at cross purposes—Steve was getting into power struggles, and Stacy was trying to appease—and neither was taking decisive action to ensure the family's safety. Once they realized this, the Robinsons developed a plan:

Family Crisis Plan: Violent Behavior

The Crisis	Our Goal	Action Steps
You say or do something that makes us feel like you'll harm someone.	To protect you and the rest of the family from harm.	We'll take this seriously. We'll walk away, including leaving the house if necessary, to give you time to cool off. We'll call 911 at any point we're not convinced you and everyone else in the family are safe.

Robert had made threats in the past but never actually harmed anyone. Nonetheless, the Robinsons felt they needed to change how they handled his threating behavior; they knew that things could someday get out of hand. They were reluctant to call 911. That's why they decided to walk away first— to give things a chance to de-escalate before having to involve outside authorities. But they were willing to call, if necessary, rather than risk someone getting hurt.

Property Theft or Damage

This category includes the threat or act of stealing or destroying highly valued property. By highly valued, we mean property that significantly contributes to the family's welfare. Damage to a cup, a broom, or a pillow might not be considered a crisis. But loss of the family car or expensive electronics could substantially impact a family's quality of life. The Martins had to deal with this kind of crisis:

> *Cathy was concerned that her daughter, Caitlyn, might take Cathy's work laptop again. Cathy worried that next time Caitlyn might damage it, erase important files, or refuse to give the computer back. When the computer was discovered missing, Cathy threatened and berated Caitlyn—saying how "ungrateful and stupid" she was to risk Cathy's job. Cathy gave Caitlyn the silent treatment for days afterward. Eventually tempers cooled down, but the incident was never discussed again; that is, until the next crisis.*

Cathy had been spending too much time criticizing her daughter and not enough time taking steps to protect her property or to meaningfully address her daughter's behavior. Cathy decided she needed a family crisis plan. Here's what she came up with:

Family Crisis Plan: Theft of or Damage to Valued Property

The Crisis	Our Goal	Action Steps
You take, destroy, or threaten to take or destroy valuable personal property.	To protect our personal property and our family's well-being.	I'll place the laptop in a lockbox and put all valuables in my locked bedroom when I leave for the day. If and when I find something valuable missing or damaged, I'll report it to the police.

Cathy's plan focuses on what *she's* going to do—a more effective approach, because Cathy's behavior is in her control. Cathy's plan also cuts down on the name-calling and yelling, which wasn't really doing any good. Instead, Cathy created consequences for Caitlyn's behavior.

Developing Your Family Crisis Plan

Having seen three different family crisis plans, now it's time to develop yours. We've provided a "Family Crisis Plan Worksheet" template at http://www. newharbinger.com/53134. It's the same worksheet the Garcias, Robinsons, and Martins used to develop their plans. Use their examples to help you decide how to word your plan. You'll need to describe (1) the crisis behavior you've decided to target, (2) your goal for dealing with the crisis, and (3) what you'll do if you encounter the crisis. Be sure to fill in all three columns.

First Column: Describing the Crisis Behavior

In deciding what crises to plan for, consider your loved one's history. Any dangerous or destructive behavior that occurs regularly requires a crisis plan, but don't forget to consider prior behavior. For example, if they were suicidal ten years ago, it might be best to plan for this kind of crisis even if it hasn't happened since.

If you feel your family's likely to encounter more than one kind of crisis behavior, you may need to write more than one plan. For each plan you write, begin by describing the crisis behavior you're targeting. Restrict the description to your loved one's behavior and how that behavior makes you feel. Resist referring to their feelings. You'd be speculating, and that's unnecessary.

Second Column: Clarifying the Goal of the Action You'll Take

Here you'll write your plan's primary goal, which clarifies your priorities for dealing with the situation and provides the rationale for the action steps you'll describe next.

Third Column: Describing the Action You'll Take

The action steps describe how you plan to respond to the crisis. Effective action steps take into account both the immediate and long-term consequences of crisis behavior. For instance, if your loved one becomes physically aggressive, you must first and foremost address any immediate threat to your family's physical well-being. Keeping your family safe is the prime objective. However, it's also wise to consider how the action steps you take now might affect the likelihood of future crises.

That's one advantage of having a plan. You're able to think things out ahead of time, consider both short- and long-term consequences, and draw clear boundaries around what you will and will not do. That reduces your risk of acting impulsively. Remember, when you act impulsively, you're more prone to accommodate and minimize, and unfortunately that increases the probability of future crises.

Take the example of a loved one threatening physical aggression. If you respond impulsively, you're likely to appease (accommodate) or challenge (minimize) them. Appeasing them makes it more likely they'll be aggressive in the future; challenging them could escalate conflict in the moment and endanger your family. Remember how the Robinsons handled their son's aggression? That's a much better option.

Additional Considerations

The crisis plan you end up developing may differ from the examples you've seen here, depending on the specific challenges you're facing, what resources are available, and other factors. You'll also need to consider goals and action steps consistent with your family's values and traditions. Whatever your plan looks like, it needs to be something you'll follow through with.

Keep in mind, a family crisis plan is not negotiable. Your loved one doesn't have to approve of or agree with your plan. *You'll* decide what qualifies as an emergency and how you plan to respond, not your loved one.

As we mentioned earlier, the decision to use an emergency service is not without controversy. It requires thoughtful planning. When 911 is called, police and ambulance involvement is likely. Depending on the nature of the crisis, emergency workers could conclude your loved one requires psychiatric hospitalization or needs to be detained or arrested. For this reason, some families are understandably hesitant to call 911. Furthermore, the quality of emergency response systems is less than optimal in some areas. Because of this, it's advisable to investigate your options ahead of time. Ask your local police department, for example, whether there are officers in your area specifically trained to deal with mental health issues. If so, you might be able to request one of the designated officers when a crisis occurs. Also, explore emergency resources other than 911 that might be available in your region.

In the end, it's your prerogative whether to involve outside authorities. Some families might prefer other resources, like extended family, close friends, or members of a religious community who're willing to assist. Whatever you decide, beware of dealing with crises on your own. It could jeopardize your family's safety and increase the likelihood you'll accommodate and minimize.

It's not always easy to determine what constitutes a crisis. Some behaviors are potentially dangerous but not currently a crisis—not yet. For example, restrictive eating, excessive alcohol intake, failure to address medical conditions, and other forms of self-neglect could all be considered a crisis in the making, even if they don't pose an immediate threat. Running away from home is sometimes a crisis behavior. If your loved one's a minor or a vulnerable adult, running away could put them at risk of serious harm.

If you're unsure whether your loved one's current or past behavior qualifies as a crisis, or if you're unclear how to respond to the crisis, get advice from a physician or other professional with the appropriate expertise to help you make that determination. They may also be able to direct you to local resources that can help you manage the kind of crisis you're anticipating. And remember our resources page: http://www.newharbinger.com/53134. There's more information there.

Be sure to develop a family crisis plan for any crisis behavior you believe you're likely to encounter. Please don't move on to step 2 before your plan's in place.

Moving Forward

Crises are not pleasant to think about, much less to plan for. However, it's wise to have a plan. Knowing what to do ahead of time is essential to escaping the family trap. But a plan is useful only if you follow it. That's what chapter 6 will help you do: implement your plan successfully.

Implementing Your Family Crisis Plan

Main Point: In this chapter, you'll implement the family crisis plan you developed in chapter 5 and learn some tips to help you follow through successfully.

You've taken the time to develop a plan. Now comes the hard part—following through. It's one thing to write your plan; it's quite another to carry it out. When a crisis arises, it's easy to forget your strategies and fall back into accommodating and minimizing. In this chapter, we'll help prepare you to implement your plan, inform your loved one about the plan, and follow through on what you've resolved to do.

Step 1 is different from the steps you'll take later. When you get to steps 2 through 5, you'll decide what changes to make and when you'll begin to make them. For example, you'll choose when to resume valued activities (step 3) and when to stop certain accommodations (step 4). What you don't get to decide is when you'll use your family crisis plan. A crisis could happen tomorrow, months from now, or never. That means you must be prepared to respond at any time.

Preparing Yourself to Follow Your Family Crisis Plan

There are many reasons families struggle to follow their plan for dealing with crises. They may panic in the moment and forget the plan. They may be too embarrassed to call the police, or reluctant to attract the attention they'd receive when an ambulance arrives. They may worry they'd humiliate their loved one or be intimidated by their loved one's aggression. All of these concerns are understandable, but they're not good reasons to abandon your plan. Why? Because if you don't follow your plan, you're likely to wing it, which means you're also likely to deal with crises by accommodating and minimizing. And that keeps you stuck in the family trap. This happened to Roy Polanski and his wife, Lynn. Roy had a plan but didn't follow it.

> *Roy planned how he'd respond if Lynn ever talked about harming herself.*
> *But when the time came, instead of taking his wife to the hospital as he'd*
> *resolved to do, Roy stayed up all night giving Lynn pep talks and*
> *monitoring her safety. As the night progressed, Roy began to wear down.*
> *He was frustrated by his failure to make Lynn feel better and resented*
> *that he was "working harder than she is." Roy pleaded with Lynn to*
> *change and then became critical of her for "giving up." The next day, Roy*
> *was upset about Lynn's behavior, and he felt guilty about how he had*
> *treated her—especially since he'd promised to act differently this time but*
> *hadn't.*

Because Roy didn't follow his plan, he resorted to accommodating and minimizing. By devoting so much attention to Lynn's crisis behavior, Roy unintentionally increased the likelihood that she'd react similarly in the future. Then he burned himself out trying to change her, which led him to minimize. Lynn felt Roy didn't understand what she was going through; she was upset that he was "so mean." And Roy's credibility was compromised. He'd told Lynn his plan but hadn't done what he'd said he'd do.

Every time you respond to recovery avoidance by accommodating and minimizing, you're increasing the likelihood your loved one will continue the same behavior in the future. And how you respond to crisis behavior is no exception. Following through with your plan—doing what you've told them you'll do—is your best chance to address your family's immediate safety and, at the same time, decrease the likelihood of future crisis behavior.

Presenting the Plan to Your Loved One

A plan is most effective when everyone involved knows what to expect. We know we've said this before, but it's an important point. When your loved one knows about the plan ahead of time, it can temper their resistance when you implement it. And it decreases the likelihood a crisis behavior will occur in the first place. For these reasons, we strongly recommend that you share the family crisis plan with your loved one.

At this point, it might be helpful to take another look at the communication guidelines (see "Telling Your Loved One About the Changes You Plan to Make," which appears in a section right before chapter 5). Follow the guidelines provided as you present the family crisis plan you developed. Introduce your plan by writing a letter; for example:

Dear _____,

As you know, I'm taking steps to change my behavior. I promised to keep you informed of the changes I plan to make.

The first thing I'm going to change is how I react to crises.

I'm going to change how I respond when you say things like "I don't want to live" or "Maybe I'd be better off dead." I used to try to cheer you up and convince you life was worth living, which didn't seem to help and made me feel resentful and lose my temper. I don't want to feel that way about you, and I don't want to treat you poorly. I just want you to be safe.

To accomplish this, I need to change my behavior. I want you to know the changes I'm planning ahead of time, so you won't be surprised. The plan is attached to this letter. Please look it over. I hope this will create a better outcome for both of us. Please let me know if you have any questions. Thanks.

Love,

_____

Now write a letter to your loved one. Use this example to help you choose your words. Once your letter's completed, attach a copy of the family crisis plan you developed in chapter 5. Then prepare to have a conversation. Set up a meeting to discuss the plan. Remember, they don't have to agree with it. Your job is simply to state how you plan to keep everyone in your family safe, including the recovery avoider.

Tips to Help You Follow Through

Now that you're committed to your plan and you've shared it with your loved one, you might find these additional tips helpful as you work to implement it.

- **Keep the plan fresh in your mind.** Look it over once a week and renew your commitment to follow it each time.

- **Get support from others if you can.** If you're having second thoughts about implementing your plan, seek consultation from a family member, friend, or professional who can provide the emotional support you need to follow through.

- **Be open to revising your plan.** If you don't feel you can follow through with your plan, consider modifying it. Revisit chapter 5, follow the instructions, and develop a new plan you're more likely to follow through with.

Moving Forward

We hope by now you've put your family crisis plan together, it's been presented to your loved one, and you're prepared to implement it whenever needed. With your plan in place, you're ready to take another step toward family well-being. Next you'll examine the impact of recovery avoidance on your life. You'll identify what valued activities to add to your life and zero in on the counterproductive behaviors you'll be scaling back. On to step 2.

Redefine the Problem

*Solutions to problems often depend
upon how they're defined.*

—Mary Catherine Bateson

CHAPTER 7

Clarifying the Impact of Recovery Avoidance on Your Life

Main Point: You'll identify the ways in which recovery avoidance has jeopardized your well-being—which could include the loss of valued activities, the addition of burdensome obligations, and the escalation of family distress. This will set the stage for you to prioritize the changes you wish to make in chapter 8.

Step 2 of the family well-being approach is about recognizing the full impact your loved one's recovery avoidance has had on your life. To do this, you must take a long, hard look at all the ways you've been affected. You'll be considering three potential negative effects—loss of valued activity, added burdensome obligations, and escalation of family distress—and the extent to which each has impacted your life. First, let's examine any valued activities you might be missing.

Impact #1: Loss of Valued Activity

People in the family trap often sacrifice things they value due to the demands of dealing with their loved one's condition. Loss of valued activity is a casualty of accommodations of omission—when you neglect endeavors that are important to you because of your loved one's impairment. It's easy to get stuck focusing on your loved one's difficulties, but in doing so, you might have neglected other things in your life that are important to you. Remember Cathy Martin, Caitlyn's mom? Let's look at what she had lost:

Cathy seldom left home because of her daughter Caitlyn's severe anxiety. Caitlyn often refused to go to school and felt she couldn't handle being alone, so Cathy started skipping her morning walks and stopped meeting her friends at the coffee shop. She also canceled her tennis lessons and stopped singing in the church choir.

Accommodations of *omission* deprive us of opportunities to relax and recharge, and that compromises our well-being (Hooker et al. 2019). Cathy noticed she was becoming increasingly tired, frustrated, and irritable. She missed how great she felt after exercising and realized how lonely she was without her friends. And though she didn't like to see Caitlyn in pain, Cathy knew that staying around her daughter 24/7 wasn't getting Caitlyn better. It was keeping the two of them captive in an exhausting holding pattern.

Are you aware of any activities you might be missing? If not, here's a list of activities that people often value. Look over the list to see if you recognize anything missing from your life.

Valued Activities You Might Be Neglecting

Relationships:

- Friends/social life (examples: going out with friends, inviting friends over, joining social clubs)

- Significant other/dating (examples: meeting new people, online dating, going out with your partner to eat, seeing a movie, and so on)

- Parenting/taking care of family (examples: feeding your family, family errands, engaging in valued activity with your immediate family)

- Extended family (examples: attending family gatherings; keeping in touch with your relatives; feeding, grooming, and playing with your pets)

Professional Life:

- Work/career (examples: time spent at your job, meetings, exploring new career options, applying for jobs)

- Volunteering/community engagement (examples: time spent volunteering, participating in civic organizations, keeping abreast of local news, getting involved in politics)

- Education, training, self-improvement (examples: taking classes, attending a public lecture, pursing a new hobby or avocation, returning to school to get a degree)

Leisure, Self-Care, Household:

- Recreation (examples: traveling, going to the theater, playing sports, pursuing hobbies)

- Religion, spirituality, reflection (examples: meditation, attending religious services, prayer, reading scripture)

- Self-care (examples: eating and sleeping well, exercising, proper hygiene, health care)

- Household responsibilities (examples: grocery shopping, cleaning, decluttering, laundry, home repairs)

Do you see any valued activities you might be neglecting, at least in part, because of your loved one? Be patient; take the time you need to consider anything you might have forgotten about. A neglected activity can be a past activity you no longer do or something you've always wanted to do but keep putting off. Remember, you can value an activity for a variety of reasons. It might bring you joy, satisfaction, pleasure, or meaning, or it might produce an outcome you value, like income or recognition.

Take a moment to list the things you'd like to do more often. They don't have to be things you'd start doing tomorrow. It can be anything you'd like to start doing sometime in the next year or so. Don't worry about restricting your list to what's most practical. Brainstorm freely and dream big; you'll prioritize where to begin in the next chapter. When you've completed your list, move on to Impact #2.

Impact # 2: Burdensome Obligations

Burdensome obligations are the result of accommodations of *commission*—those extra responsibilities you've taken on to compensate for your loved one's impairment. Cathy Martin, for instance, did a lot of things for Caitlyn: writing notes to excuse her daughter's absences from school, doing Caitlyn's household chores, and prompting Caitlyn to get out of bed, bathe, eat, and do her homework—just to name a few.

Most of us have enough to contend with in life without the additional burdens that come from accommodating recovery avoidance. Accommodations of commission add another layer of burden to all the other obligations and responsibilities you face. It's easy to feel overwhelmed, as Cathy did: guilty for lying to the school, resentful of serving Caitlyn in her room, and exhausted by responding to Caitlyn's constant requests for reassurance.

Not all accommodations are created equal. It's the ones that directly interfere with your life or are inconsistent with your values—your sense of right or wrong—that most often compromise your well-being and create resentment. Not surprisingly, they're also the ones most likely to lead you to minimize. This is an important point. You'll soon be deciding which accommodations to stop, and you should prioritize the accommodations that are particularly detrimental to your well-being.

Cathy took this into account when considering which accommodations to discontinue. She decided to continue cooking healthy meals for her daughter. She enjoyed doing so and didn't resent it. But there were other things Cathy *did* resent—like delivering meals to Caitlyn's bedroom, writing notes to the school, and reminding Caitlyn to do things. These were accommodations Cathy planned to stop.

You've seen Cathy's accommodations and the burdens they represent. What accommodations do you provide your loved one? Which ones do you find particularly burdensome? To help you think this out, here's a list of accommodations commonly practiced by families dealing with recovery avoidance:

Common Accommodating Behaviors

- Assisting your loved one to complete essential tasks (examples: doing their laundry, running errands for them, making phone calls on their behalf, making excuses for them to others)

- Assisting your loved one to complete nonessential tasks (examples: participating in compulsive rituals, repeating a completed task to meet their perfectionistic or idiosyncratic standards, complying with their unreasonable or nonsensical requests)

- Repeatedly providing reassurance (examples: assuring them something is safe or that it was done right, reciting a specific phrase to make them feel better, reassuring them about their appearance or performance)

- Restricting what you say or do (examples: walking on eggshells, not bringing up topics that might upset them, avoiding doing things they have told you not to do)

- Making exceptions to normal family rules (examples: tolerating behavior you normally wouldn't from others; allowing your loved one to bow out of family gatherings; permitting them to leave messes around the house, make noise late at night, get out of household chores, spend family money on nonessential things, and so on)

- Providing financial support (examples: paying for expenses you wouldn't normally provide for other adult family members—car payments, computers, rent)

Were you able to identify the responsibilities and obligations you've assumed in your effort to accommodate your loved one? How does each interfere with your life? Consider the cost of the behavior—the time or money you spend doing it, the impact on your relationships (with your loved one or with others), the emotional and physical impact, and anything else you recognize. Are you aware of how you feel about having to provide these accommodations? Which ones would you like to stop someday? Write them down. Be sure to include any you identify, even if they don't appear on this list.

You've now examined two ways recovery avoidance might have affected your life. There's one more to consider—the distress you and your family experience.

Impact #3: Escalation of Family Distress

The escalation of family distress is, at least in part, the result of minimizing behavior. Cathy's interactions with Caitlyn illustrate how this plays out. When Cathy became tired of accommodating Caitlyn, she'd get upset—often raising her voice, saying things like, "Can't you just deal with this?" or calling her names and insulting her. At other times, Cathy would try to cajole Caitlyn, prodding her to go to school by repeatedly reminding Caitlyn about the importance of education. In the end, none of it worked. In fact, the two of them usually wound up frustrated and angry at one another.

When you minimize, you're contributing to the escalation of family distress. Cathy didn't intend to make things worse. No one does. But when Cathy yelled at Caitlyn, Caitlyn yelled back, further aggravating Cathy. From Caitlyn's perspective, her mother's yelling and pleading was further evidence that her mother didn't recognize the severity of Caitlyn's anxiety, leaving Caitlyn feeling misunderstood and defensive. Cathy and Caitlyn were caught in an emotional tug-of-war.

Having seen what happens in the Martin family, can you identify similar patterns in your family—times when minimizing hinders your relationship with your loved one and escalates the conflict between you? To help you recognize the ways in which you might be minimizing, take a moment to look over some common minimizing behaviors.

Common Minimizing Behaviors:

Providing reminders	Coaching/lecturing
Cheerleading	Criticizing
Dismissing another person's fears or concerns	Telling someone why they should get help
Name-calling	Yelling
Pointing out the good things in a person's life	Questioning another person's motives
Threatening or pressuring	Rolling your eyes
Sighing heavily	Physical aggression
Shaming	Guilting
Nagging	The silent treatment
Telling them "it's not that bad"	

Anything look familiar? If you're reluctant to acknowledge the ways you minimize, that's understandable. Minimizing isn't always pretty. But it's pretty normal for anyone who's been in a family trap for any length of time. Please be honest with yourself. You can't find a solution if you don't see the problem, and a critical part of the problem is the tension that happens between you and the recovery avoider in your life.

Write down any minimizing behaviors you recognize are relevant to you. And once you're done, try not to be too self-critical. Minimizing is nothing to be ashamed of. As we've said repeatedly, it's part of the natural response to recovery avoidance, something family members ultimately do when a loved one's condition affects their lives. Give yourself credit. You're acknowledging the things you want to change and devoting the effort needed to make it happen. And that takes insight and courage.

Moving Forward

You've now evaluated the three ways in which recovery avoidance might have negatively affected you and your family. That means you recognize the valued activities you've lost, the burdens you've endured by accommodating, and how your minimizing contributes to family distress. In the process, you've identified changes you'd like to make in your life. Congratulations! You've redefined the problem. The problem is no longer your loved one's condition. It's how your loved one's behavior affects you and how you respond to it. That's what you're going to change—that's in your control.

Of course, now you must decide exactly where to begin. That's next, in chapter 8.

Prioritizing the Changes You Want to Make

Main Point: You'll decide where to begin making changes. That includes what valued activity to start and what accommodating and minimizing behaviors you most want to stop.

In chapter 7, you redefined the problem. Now it's time to set goals based on your priorities. Not goals for your loved one, but goals for changing your own behavior and improving your well-being. You'll focus on obtainable goals, things you can control—like reclaiming those neglected valued activities, lessening your burden by withdrawing accommodations, and easing family distress by scaling back your minimizing.

Let's Get Started

Looking at all the potential changes you could make might feel overwhelming. Please don't let that stop you. You won't do everything at once—and you shouldn't even try. Take it one step at a time. And build on your successes as you go. We'll help you narrow your focus by clarifying your priorities on a worksheet entitled "Changes I Intend to Make First," which you can download from http://www.newharbinger.com/53134. First up: selecting which valued activity to start with.

Prioritizing the Valued Activity You're Going to Start

Look over the neglected valued activities you identified in chapter 7, and consider which activity is most important to you. Perhaps it's something you used to do or something you've wanted to do but kept putting it off. If, for some reason, you anticipate that your first choice is going to be too difficult—for example, you anticipate significant pushback from your loved one—feel free to pick something less challenging, as long as it's something you value doing.

Use the Changes I Intend to Make First worksheet. In the section entitled "Valued Activities I'd Like to Start," write the first activity you've decided to start in row one. Then write any other activities you'd like to start in the second row.

Prioritizing the Accommodations You're Going to Stop

Families dealing with recovery avoidance are sometimes tempted to stop providing a "foundational" accommodation—that is, one that provides an individual with basic necessities of life, like food, shelter, or health care. Threats to remove a foundational accommodation usually occur in the heat of the moment, during intense family conflict. As you can imagine, taking action like kicking your loved one out of the house or terminating their health insurance—comes with great risks. It can jeopardize their physical safety and accelerate turmoil and conflict within the family. For these reasons, removing a foundational accommodation should be your last resort, and it should never be initiated impulsively. If you're seriously considering removing a foundational accommodation, be sure to read chapter 15 before you decide. It tells you when to consider it and what you should know before doing it.

More than likely, like most of the families we work with, you'll be focusing on removing situational accommodations—the accommodations of commission you read about in chapter 7. Situational accommodations are attempts to help a loved one with the challenges presented by a specific situation, like doing laundry, getting up in the morning, or driving to the store. Withdrawing this kind of assistance may be inconvenient or uncomfortable for your loved one but is typically not dangerous and poses no serious threat to anyone's survival. Unlike removing a foundational accommodation, when families discontinue situational accommodations, they're more likely to follow through successfully.

Now it's time to select which accommodations you want to withdraw first. Return to the list of accommodations you wrote down in chapter 7, the ones you felt were relevant to your life. As you prioritize, there are a couple of things to consider. Some families begin with the accommodations that impact them the most. Others prefer to withdraw accommodations they believe will generate the least resistance from their loved one. Eventually, you'll want to target all accommodations that are burdensome for you. It's your best chance to improve family well-being. However, what's most important now is to follow your plan, whatever it is. Following through now establishes your credibility for the future. So whatever you select, be prepared to carry it out.

Return to your worksheet ("Changes I Intend to Make First"). In the section entitled "Accommodating Behaviors I'd Like to Stop," write in row one the accommodating behavior you've decided to stop first. Then write any other accommodating behaviors you'd like to stop in row two.

Prioritizing the Minimizing You're Going to Stop

Review the list of minimizing behaviors you identified in chapter 7, the ones you felt were relevant to you. Once again, you'll need to decide where to begin. In a perfect world, you'd eliminate minimizing altogether. But that's probably not realistic. Begin by concentrating on the behavior that happens most often or that causes the most conflict between you and your loved one. Are there things you say or do that consistently set them off? Is there something in particular they complain about the most?

Return to the worksheet ("Changes I Intend to Make First") and in the section "Minimizing Behaviors I'd Like to Stop," write the first behavior you'd like to stop in row one. In the second row, write any other minimizing behaviors you'd like to stop.

A Note of Caution

Be careful not to underestimate the impact your loved one's behavior has had on your life. Families dealing with recovery avoidance notoriously ignore their own needs. When your attention's been disproportionately focused on someone else, it's easy to lose touch with your own suffering. Before proceeding to the next step, be sure you've thoroughly considered any valued activities you might be missing, all the burdens you endure by accommodating, and the subtle and not-so-subtle ways you might be minimizing. If your life is negatively impacted and you don't recognize it, it will be harder to escape the family trap. Try asking for input from family members and others who know you well. What have they noticed, and how do they view your interactions with recovery avoidance? They may see something you don't.

Moving Forward

With this chapter, you've completed step 2 of the program. You've identified where you'll begin your effort to embrace valued activity and reduce accommodating and minimizing. In the chapters ahead, you'll make those changes happen. First up is step 3, the pursuit of valued activity.

Embrace Valued Activity

I have come to believe that caring for myself is not self-indulgent. Caring for myself is an act of survival.

—Audre Lorde

Precheck: Do I Need Step 3?

You need step 3 if: You've been neglecting activity that's important to your well-being.

You might skip step 3 if: There are no significant pleasurable or meaningful activities you're currently neglecting because of your loved one.

Risks of skipping step 3: If you downplay the importance of valued activities you've let slip away, it could jeopardize your emotional well-being and impair your ability to take the remaining steps outlined in this book.

If you skip step 3: Be cautious and self-aware. Return to this step if you later realize there are valued activities you've missed.

CHAPTER 9

Developing Your Plan to Embrace Valued Activity

Main Point: In this chapter, you'll develop a plan to incorporate activities you value into your life. The plan will include what you're going to do, how often, and when and where.

As you develop your plan, keep in mind that the emphasis is now on you, not on your loved one. That means you'll work on finding ways to live your life as fully and productively as possible. Still not convinced this is important? Consider rereading chapter 4 to make sure you're not succumbing to one of those toxic myths we mentioned. Stress of any kind is easier to endure when you're fortified by things that bring you joy, meaning, and productivity; that can give you the emotional strength you'll need to escape the family trap. But first, you need a plan to make this happen.

Let's Get Started

Planning for behavior change can help you follow through more consistently. It can serve as a check on your tendency to expect too little or too much of yourself. It also helps you anticipate things that might get in your way and allows you to problem solve ahead of time. Take a moment to familiarize yourself with the worksheet you'll be using.

The Valued Activity Plan worksheet (find it at http://www.newharbinger.com/53134) has five columns. We're focusing now on the first two columns—one for what you're planning to do and another for when you plan to do it.

Valued Activity Plan

What I Plan to Do	
Activity	When

You'll use this form to organize your plan to increase valued activity. There's another half of the form (not shown here), labeled "Did I Do It?" But don't worry about that for now. We'll go over that in chapter 10 when you're monitoring your performance. For now, focus on developing your plan.

Before going further, let's see what Roy Polanski's plan looked like. Remember Roy and his family from the Introduction and chapter 6? Roy had been spending a lot of time driving his wife, Lynn, to medical visits for her undiagnosed illnesses and checking up on her at home. As a consequence, Roy felt he no longer had time to exercise, an activity he valued greatly. Here are some of Roy's considerations as he developed his plan:

- He knew attempting to do too much at once, at least at first, would be harder to follow through with, so he began by incorporating one activity into his daily routine: He'd resume walking regularly.

- He also considered the number of days he'd walk, which days, the best time to walk, and how long he'd walk, taking into account his current physical condition and the other demands on his time. Roy knew he'd become out of shape and needed to take it easy at first. He decided to start with after-dinner evening walks, gradually building up over time. He initially considered walking early in the morning but knew he'd have difficulty getting out of bed on time. Expecting more of himself early in the mornings could set him up for failure.

- Considering his previous attempts to make changes, Roy realized it often helped him to be accountable to others, so he invited a friend to walk with him. This would make the walks more enjoyable and give Roy built-in motivation to follow through.

- Roy's initial plan was to walk in the park, but he needed a backup plan for challenging weather conditions, which was walking at the mall—not as enjoyable as walking in the park, but a reasonable alternative in bad weather.

Here's Roy's first valued activity plan:

What I Plan to Do	
Activity	When
Walk for 20 minutes at Button Park	Monday, 7 p.m.
	Wednesday, 7 p.m.
	Friday, 7 p.m.

You may be thinking this kind of planning is unnecessary or a waste of time. But behavioral research tells us that planning—thinking out where to begin, anticipating obstacles, and committing to a predetermined time schedule—is the most effective way to make changes in our behavior, and, more important, to make those changes last (Stein et al. 2021).

Now it's time to plan the changes you'll make by completing your own valued activity plan. Refer to the "Changes I Intend to Make First" worksheet you completed in chapter 8, where you listed the neglected valued activity you intend to start first. Begin with one valued activity. Describe it in the first column of your Valued Activity Plan worksheet. Enter when you're going to do it—both the day of the week and the time of day—in the second column.

Behavior change is more reliable if you anticipate potential obstacles that might keep you from following through. This is an important part of the planning process. It can be the difference in whether your plan succeeds or not. Let's see how Roy did this:

Roy recognized he tends to forget things when he's stressed. And he knew the days Lynn was especially anxious tended to leave him itching for ways to relax and turn his mind off—typically, turning on the TV—which kept him from doing things that might've been more productive. He also knew he needed to be prepared; he reasoned that even something as mundane as forgetting his walking shoes or water bottle might give him an excuse not to walk. He also knew he'd prefer to walk outside, even if it was lightly raining, rather than walk in the mall—which meant he'd need a raincoat.

After identifying the obstacles he might encounter, Roy listed steps he could take to get around each obstacle. Here's what he came up with:

The Steps I Need to Take to Make My Plan Happen
Put my walking shoes, water bottle, and raincoat in my car. Leave them there.
Schedule day and time on my phone. Add an alarm one hour before.
Write reminders to myself to keep my commitment—including one I'll tape to the TV remote so I'm not tempted to slack off.

As you can see, Roy was able to think of at least one way to overcome each of the obstacles he identified. We hope seeing Roy's plan helped you think about what you need to do to make your plan happen.

Now it's time to think about your own plan. Is there anything you think might get in your way? If so, see if you can develop a strategy to address the obstacles you anticipate. Write your strategies down so you don't forget them.

When Your Loved One Resists

Your pursuit of valued activity could be met with resistance. It depends on how your loved one perceives the changes you're trying to make. If those changes don't significantly impact them, you're unlikely to encounter opposition. However, if they see what you're doing as a threat, you may have to deal with some form of protest. Suppose the activity you're pursuing makes you less available to provide accommodations, or presents a situation they struggle with, like having guests in the house. If you encounter resistance, try not to let it stop you altogether. Consider an alternative activity you could initiate for now, one that might meet less resistance. You can always return to your original choice later. If the resistance escalates into crisis behavior, please implement your family crisis plan. (And if you don't have one, please return to chapters 5 and 6 and make one.)

Moving Forward

By now, you should have a plan to initiate one valued activity. Your plan should include the activity you'll begin doing, when you'll do it, and the steps you need to take to make it happen. Now it's time to put your plan into action. On to chapter 10.

Implementing Your Plan to Embrace Valued Activity

Main Point: In this chapter, you'll implement the plan you developed in chapter 9. You'll learn how to follow through successfully and how to modify your plan as you go along.

As you carry out your plan, remember that even small changes can be difficult. There's no way to predict all the challenges you might encounter. Don't worry; you'll be able to adjust your plan along the way. Also keep in mind that embracing valued activity is an ongoing process. You'll be able to add more activities later, especially as each activity you initiate becomes part of your routine.

Let's Get Started

Before starting your valued activity plan, we'll show you how to keep a record of your performance, evaluate how well you did, modify your plan as needed, and take steps to maintain your plan in the future. But first you'll decide whether to tell your loved one what you plan to do.

Do I Need to Inform My Loved One About My Plan?

If your pursuit of valued activity doesn't directly impact your loved one, there may be little need to announce what you're doing. It's your life, after all. However, if you think they may feel threatened by the changes you're about to make, it's best to share your plan ahead of time.

Roy knew that if he started exercising again, he'd be less available to Lynn when she needed a ride or wanted immediate reassurance about her medical symptoms. He felt he had to tell her what he was about to do, so she could prepare to work around his schedule. Roy put his thoughts in writing:

Dear Lynn:

As you know, I have been trying to improve both how I treat you and our family's well-being, which requires that I take better care of myself. I am going to start exercising again. My current plan is to walk in the park three evenings a week. I have attached my exercise schedule to this letter so you will know when I will not be available.

I hope to make further changes in the future and will try to keep you updated each time, especially if it's something that might affect you.

Love,

Roy

Roy's letter is well written. It's respectful of Lynn, with no minimizing comments. His objective is clearly stated—he's trying to improve his own well-being, not inconvenience Lynn. And he's promising to keep her informed of any future changes.

Do you think the activity changes you're planning will affect your loved one? If so, consider writing a letter similar to Roy's. Be sure to attach your Valued Activity Plan worksheet.

After you've written the letter, set up a meeting with your loved one. If you feel it'd be helpful, review the communication guidelines in "Telling Your Loved One About the Changes You Plan to Make" before conducting your meeting. These are the same guidelines you followed when you presented your family crisis plan.

Keeping a Record of Your Performance

It's helpful to monitor how well your plan is working. That allows you to make adjustments along the way. To do this, you'll use the right half of the Valued Activity Plan worksheet, the one you downloaded from http://www.newharbinger.com/53134. You're already familiar with the "What I Plan to

Do" section, which you filled out in chapter 9. You'll use the "Did I Do It?" section to evaluate how well you followed through.

Did I Do It?		
Yes	No	If Not, What I Did Instead

For each activity, you'll place a checkmark in the "Yes" column if you completed that activity, or the "No" column if you didn't. In the third column, "If Not, What I Did Instead," you'll document what you did instead if you deviated from your plan.

Roy used this form to monitor his performance. Recall that he wanted to walk for twenty minutes at Button Park on Monday, Wednesday, and Friday at 7:00 p.m. Let's see how he did.

What I Plan to Do			
Activity			
Walk for 20 mins at Button Park			
Did I Do It?			
	Yes	No	If Not, What I Did Instead
Mon 7 p.m		X	Went to my dentist appointment and forgot about when I scheduled the walk.
Wed 7 p.m.	X		
Fri 7 p.m.		X	Went home. Watched TV with Lynn.

Roy had some success, but there's room for improvement. He followed his plan on Wednesday but missed Monday and Friday.

Use the form as Roy did to monitor how well you implement your valued activity plan. If at all possible, fill it out right after you complete the activity, when it's fresh in your mind. If you happen to forget, try to complete the form as soon after the activity as possible. You'll need an accurate record of your performance to evaluate it effectively. Monitor your performance for one week.

Evaluating Your Performance

Now let's see how you did. Were you able to follow your plan successfully? If you nailed it the first time out, congratulations! Simply follow the same plan next week. Or maybe even add an activity if you like. Just be careful not to do too much at once.

If you stumbled a bit, as Roy did, don't be too discouraged. Changing behavior and building new habits can be difficult. The most effective way to improve performance requires the right balance between honest self-examination and thoughtful self-compassion. Be willing to acknowledge when you fall short of your goals, without wasting time putting yourself down. Self-criticism won't help you solve the problem; identifying what got in your way will.

Figuring Out What Got in Your Way

There's always a reason people don't do what they set out to do. Before they can correct their performance, they must first identify what got them off track. Roy figured out what got in his way:

- *I forgot to look at my schedule to check for appointments that might interfere with my plan to walk. When I failed to walk on Monday, I intended to make it up on Tuesday, but it was raining hard outside and traffic getting to the mall was very heavy.*

- *I felt tired and demotivated after work on Friday. I stayed up late on Thursday night, which likely contributed to my fatigue.*

Did anything get in your way? Maybe you didn't spend enough time preparing for the activity. Perhaps you were distracted by some other priority.

Maybe you forgot about it because of other things going on in your life. What was it that interfered with your follow-through? Take a moment to think about what got in your way. Write your thoughts down. Of course, knowing what got in your way won't do you much good if you don't find a way around it.

Addressing Whatever Got in Your Way

Once you know what got in your way, you'll be able to make appropriate adjustments to your next valued activity plan. There are two basic ways to correct your plan: choose a less difficult activity, or plan the same activity but add strategies to address whatever got in your way.

Roy decided to make his exercise goal less difficult.

Roy worked at least forty hours per week, Monday through Friday, and sometimes had after-work appointments. In addition, unanticipated demands on his time would crop up regularly. And, of course, the work of managing Lynn's condition also impacted his schedule. He decided to schedule two walks per week instead of three, at least to start—lowering the bar to make the commitment easier to keep. Roy also planned to look ahead at his calendar at the beginning of each week to avoid scheduling walks on the same days as other appointments. And he decided to schedule one walk on the weekend, when work wouldn't interfere. Roy decided that once he could follow through with two walks per week for at least a month, he would add additional exercise.

Roy made his plan easier, but Steve Robinson took another route: He developed a strategy to address what got in his way.

Steve, who'd been struggling to play tennis once a week, decided to keep his original goal. He called his friend Jim to invite him to play. Jim was unable to play, so Steve put up a notice at the tennis club looking for a partner. He received no calls for over a week, so he paid for lessons with a tennis coach for a few weeks during his planned times. He reasoned that getting back to the tennis club and working with a coach would help him meet other people to play tennis with regularly. The obligation of having to pay the tennis coach also felt like an incentive to keep his commitment. Additionally, Steve began inviting his daughter, Olivia, to the tennis club on Saturday mornings and taking her out to lunch after. That gave him time with Olivia and gave her a break from the stress of being at home with her brother, Robert, during the weekend.

Which option is best for you? Will you plan a less difficult activity or do something to address the things that got in your way? Once you've decided, you'll be able to make the right corrections to your next valued activity plan.

Developing Your Next Valued Activity Plan

Once you've evaluated your performance, you can make your next valued activity plan. If you followed your initial plan successfully, you may not need any changes in the next one—except, of course, adding another activity if you wish.

If you struggled to follow your plan, we hope you were able to identify what you're going to do differently next time. Be sure your next plan addresses the obstacles that got in your way the week before. Be careful not to add any new activities until you're able to follow your current plan successfully. When you're ready to make your next valued activity plan, get another copy of the worksheet (http://www.newharbinger.com/53134) and fill it in to reflect whatever changes you've decided to make.

Maintaining Your Plan in the Future

Once you've successfully followed through with one or two planned activities, begin adding additional activities as you wish. Consider all the valued activities you identified in step 2. Add them to your weekly plan as you feel ready to take on more. It's probably best, though, to add one activity at a time.

Embracing valued activity is not a short-term project. Hopefully, you'll be tweaking your valued activity plan for the rest of your life. There'll be challenges along the way and obstacles that may temporarily throw you off your path. So here are a few tips to help you maintain a life of valued activity:

- **Plan ahead.** Look at your calendar and anticipate planned events that might compete with your planned valued activity. Make adjustments as appropriate.

- **Have a plan for dealing with those days you "just don't feel like it."** You may feel excessively tired, stressed, or overwhelmed. Plan for what you can do or say to yourself to help you get started. For instance, you can remind yourself of the goals and values that prompted you to increase valued activity. You can remind yourself of previous times you've felt better after getting started.

- **Be willing to modify an activity to make it less difficult.** This is sometimes necessary to jump-start your progress. Something's better than nothing. At least it heads you in the right direction.

- **Reward yourself for a job well done.** For instance, you could allocate yourself a certain amount of money each time you follow through. That money could go toward something special you can earn only by following through with your planned tasks.

- **If rewards don't work, consider penalties.** For instance, you could commit to sending a predetermined amount of money to a charity or organization each time you don't follow through. Sometimes people choose a charity or organization they'd rather not support to give themselves some extra incentive.

- **Don't waste time criticizing yourself.** Save your mental energy to solve problems, to figure out what's holding you back and how to get around it.

- **Be ready to use your family crisis plan if necessary.** Keep it handy.

- **Seek professional help if you think you need it.** The very issues that contribute to recovery avoidance can also hinder your efforts. A mental health clinician may be able to keep them from holding you back.

If at any point you struggle with the pursuit of valued activity, do what Roy and Steve did—examine what got in your way and determine how to get around it. That's the key to embracing valued activity in the long run.

Moving Forward

You have your plan in place, and hopefully you've had a chance to see how well it's working. If you're struggling to follow through, use our suggestions to modify your plan and try it again. It's important to enhance your well-being by doing the things that bring you pleasure and meaning. You're about to move to step 4, where you'll be making big changes in how you approach your loved one. You'll probably need all the emotional strength you can get—and the valued activities you've embraced can be a big step in that direction.

Ease Family Distress

If you can do no good, at least do no harm.

—Kurt Vonnegut

Precheck: Do I Need Step 4?

You need step 4 if: (1) You provide accommodations to your loved one *and/or* (2) you engage in minimizing behavior when you interact with them.

You might skip step 4 if: (1) You're *not* accommodating your loved one in any significant way *and* (2) you're *not* engaging in minimizing behavior when you interact with them.

Risks of skipping step 4: As you've already learned, accommodating and minimizing make recovery avoidance worse and jeopardize your well-being. If you're doing either and don't recognize it, you may be unable to escape the family trap.

If you skip step 4: You can skip to step 5, but beware. It's rare when no accommodating or minimizing is going on. Keep an eye out for any counter-productive behavior you might have missed. If you discover something, return to step 4 and read chapters 11 and 12.

CHAPTER 11

Developing Your Plan to Ease Family Distress

Main Point: You'll develop a plan to lessen conflict and stress in the family by changing your behavior. You'll identify alternative ways to respond to your loved one that don't include accommodating and minimizing. By the end of this chapter, you'll have a written plan describing how and when you'll begin your next step out of the family trap.

In step 3, you targeted behavior you want to do more of. We hope you were able to make that happen. In step 4, you'll focus on behavior you want to do less of—accommodating and minimizing. You'll be exploring new ways to interact with your loved one that will ease the distress in your family.

Let's Get Started

Consider how much your accommodating and minimizing contribute to family distress. When you accommodate, you acquire additional burdens, which increases your distress. When that happens, you're more likely to minimize, which increases your loved one's distress. When their distress increases, recovery avoidance worsens, and so does the pressure for you to accommodate. And so on and so on. It's a trap in which everyone is stuck. Accommodating increases *your* distress. Minimizing increases *their* distress.

When you cut back on both, everyone benefits. But to make that happen, you're going to need a family well-being plan.

Developing the Family Well-Being Plan

We've developed a worksheet to help you organize your attempts to reduce accommodating and minimizing. The Family Well-Being Plan worksheet, available at http://www.newharbinger.com/53134, is divided into two main parts—The Problem and The Solution.

Part 1: The Problem
The Situation:
How I've Been Responding:
Part 2: The Solution
How I Plan to Treat You Better:
How I Plan to Treat Myself Better:
Start Date:

Using the worksheet, you'll describe a problematic situation, the counterproductive ways you used to respond, how you're going to treat your loved one better in the future, how you're going to treat yourself better in the future, and the date the plan will start.

If there are other family members trying to escape the family trap with you, they may need to complete their own family well-being plan. Not everyone accommodates and minimizes in the same way, and each person's relationship with the recovery avoider is specific to them.

Now let's walk through each task necessary to develop an effective family well-being plan. You'll begin by identifying which problematic situation you'd like to address first.

Task 1: Identify One Problematic Situation

A problematic situation is any interaction between you and your loved one that interferes with your life. Most often it's when their agenda clashes with yours and creates conflict. Problematic situations are when you're most likely to accommodate and minimize. They're the petri dish in which the family trap develops. Here are few examples:

- For Vivienne and Andrew Chen, it's their mother's demand for a visit from the grandkids. They want their mother to see her grandchildren, but grandma has a hoarding problem, and the house is unsafe.

- For Roy Polanski, it's his wife's constant requests to be reassured that she's not dying. He wants to ease his wife's anxiety, but his answers never seem to satisfy her, and he always winds up resentful.

- For Sara Garcia, it's her husband's struggle to attend family events. She misses him when he's not there, and she wants him to be part of family life. She dreads the battle she'll endure trying to get him out of the house, but she's tired of showing up without him and having to make excuses to the rest of the family.

- For Cathy Martin, it's her daughter's refusal to come to the dinner table. Cathy wants to have a normal family dinner, but the effort to get her daughter to the table usually ends in a fight.

Let's examine in more detail a problematic situation that happens often between Rachel Goldberg and her husband, Sam, who has OCD and struggles with checking compulsions. Their situation helps to illustrate the tasks of developing a family well-being plan:

When it's time to leave the house, Sam feels extremely anxious and has a strong urge to check that all the doors and windows are locked, all the appliances are turned off, and nothing is left out that could potentially harm the family pet. His checking can easily take an hour, and sometimes a lot longer. Rachel gets frustrated with Sam and reacts strongly at times, alternating between accommodating (helping Sam complete checking rituals, reassuring him nothing bad will happen) and minimizing (expressing frustration, lecturing, and yelling). Later Rachel feels guilty for treating Sam poorly.

This—Sam's checking behavior before he leaves the house, and Rachel's drive to accommodate or minimize when this happens—was the problematic situation she chose to work on. Here's how she summarized the problematic situation:

Part 1: The Problem

The Situation: You continue checking to make sure doors and windows are locked and appliances are off when it's time for us to leave the house.

Note how Rachel's language is clear and nonjudgmental. It took a few drafts for her to arrive at a description of Sam's behavior that was free of criticism and judgment. Her first draft stated, "You always get stuck in compulsions when we're trying to leave the house, and you end up making me late. I'm sick and tired of it." She felt justified saying these things. But when Rachel later looked at what she had written, she could see how her statements might come across as judgmental and could make Sam defensive. Rachel recognized that her frustration was seeping into what could have been a more neutral description of Sam's behavior. Realizing she needed to edit out the minimizing, Rachel wrote a second draft that was less likely to make Sam feel defensive.

You've seen Rachel's example. Now it's your turn. Which problematic situations would you like to change, and where would you like to begin? Think about the counterproductive behaviors you identified on your priorities worksheet ("Changes I Intend to Make First"). Ask yourself: *In what situations are those behaviors most likely to occur?* That should help narrow down your options.

One caution: Be careful not to be too ambitious, which can make following through more difficult. Although you might be eager to start with the situation that's most problematic, it's better to start with a less complicated, more manageable situation, one you believe won't elicit too much pushback from your loved one. And although you might want to tackle multiple problems at once, starting with only one situation—at least to begin with—increases the chances that your efforts will pay off. And remember the importance of follow-through: Whatever you include in your initial family well-being plan, be sure you're ready to do it. It's better to implement a modest change that you're ready to follow through with than to attempt a more ambitious plan you won't be able to carry out. You'll be able to take on greater challenges later on. (Chapter 12 provides guidelines for deciding when to add additional problematic situations to the plan.)

Once you've identified the problematic situation you'll be addressing first, enter it on the "The Situation" row of your Family Well-Being Plan worksheet. Try to emulate how Rachel described Sam's behavior—sticking to the facts, as best you can, without letting feelings or judgments filter in. As Rachel did, describe your loved one's behavior ("You continue checking") and the problem it creates for you ("when it's time to leave the house"). Then move on to task #2.

Task 2: Identify the Counterproductive Ways You Used to Respond

The second row, "How I've Been Responding," is for you to describe your contributions to the problematic situation. Here you'll summarize any accommodating and minimizing you do (or perhaps used to do) in that situation. Here's Rachel's description:

Part 1: The Problem
The Situation: You continue checking to make sure doors and windows are locked and appliances are off when it's time to leave the house.
How I've Been Responding: I sometimes yell at you. I tell you "We need to go now." I lecture you. I try to reassure you that nothing bad will happen while we are gone. I help with your checking to try to get you to move faster, but I do it in a way that shows how frustrated I feel at that moment. The next day, I sometimes yell at you and then apologize for overreacting.

Notice that Rachel's description includes both how she accommodates and how she minimizes. She even included how she sometimes minimizes (yelling at Sam) after the situation has passed.

Can you identify how you accommodate and minimize in your problematic situation? If so, describe your behavior in the second row ("How I've Been Responding"). Use Rachel's example to guide you. Be sure to include all accommodating and minimizing behavior relevant to the situation; that includes minimizing behavior that occurs later on.

You've now identified the problem. That's crucial. Now we can move on to the solution.

Task 3: Identify How You're Going to Treat Your Loved One Better

Task 3 involves deciding what you'll do instead of minimizing—how you plan to treat your loved one better. This might seem simple, but easier said than done when it comes to dealing with recovery avoidance. When you've been in a family trap for a long time, it's common to lose sight of any other way to respond. Even if you know what you ought to do, your loved one's behavior can trigger strong emotions that can quickly lead you back into minimizing. So it's important to decide what you'll do ahead of time, spell it out in your plan, and prepare to follow through.

On the "Changes I Intend to Make First" worksheet, you've identified the minimizing behavior you plan to stop first. Of course, you can decide to focus on more than one minimizing behavior at a time. Just notice whether you are successful, and narrow your approach if you need to.

Stopping a counterproductive behavior is more likely to succeed if you know what to replace it with. The alternative to counterproductive behavior is, of course, productive behavior. A behavior is productive if it produces the desired outcome. And the desired outcome for someone in the family trap is to escape: to no longer be stuck in a situation in which their hope for the future rests largely on their loved one's behavior. For those dealing with recovery avoidance, a behavior is productive—contributes to the desired outcome—if it promotes the well-being of one or more family members without making recovery avoidance worse.

To help you come up with productive alternatives to minimizing behavior, we've provided a table that clarifies the differences between counterproductive and productive behavior.

Counterproductive Behavior	Productive Behavior
• Focuses on things you can't control	• Focuses on things you can control
• Tries to get your loved one to do something	• Is about what you will or will not do
• Leads you into power struggles	• Helps you stay out of power struggles
• Is spontaneous	• Is strategic, based on a plan
• Responds to the immediate situation	• Considers the long-term outcome
• Is poorly communicated	• Is spelled out clearly ahead of time
• Is inconsistent or sporadic	• Is consistent

Now let's see a few specific examples. The next table offers a productive alternative for each of the most common minimizing behaviors.

Minimizing Behaviors	Productive Alternatives
• Yelling	• Speaking in a calm voice
• Nagging	• Making a request—once
• Lecturing	• Making a point—once
• Criticizing	• Empathizing
• Arguing	• Leaving the room
• Accusing	• Asking—once
• Threatening	• Setting limits
• Being verbally defensive	• Staying silent
• Re-explaining why you're doing something	• Doing something without comment

Can you see the advantages of each productive behavior on the right—how it would be less likely to escalate conflict between you and your loved one? As you consider how you'll treat them better, take some time to review the general characteristics of productive behavior and look over the specific examples we've provided. Let's see how Rachel planned to treat Sam better.

Part 2: The Solution
How I Plan to Treat You Better: I am going to refrain from lecturing you or yelling at you. I plan to talk to you gently and respectfully instead. I'll let you know the time we are supposed to leave and invite you to come with me. But if you're unable to make it, I'll understand and won't be upset with you.

Note how Rachel plans to speak calmly to Sam without criticism and judgment. She's told Sam what she will and will not do, identifying the minimizing she intends to stop and the productive behavior she intends to start. She may still feel upset and frustrated on days when Sam's symptoms make it too hard for him to leave the house without checking, but she's committed to not expressing this to him in ways that will keep them both stuck in the family trap, as they have been for so long.

It's your turn now. Mindful of the things you've learned, decide how you'll treat your love one better. Enter it in the "How I Plan to Treat You Better" section of the worksheet. Then move on to the next task. Family well-being means treating yourself better too.

Task 4: Identify How You're Going to Treat Yourself Better

You've described how you'll treat your loved one better; now it's time to treat yourself better. That means mapping out how you'll withdraw the accommodations that burden you. This is a vital part of improving your well-being. Think about how you've accommodated your loved one in the problematic situation identified on your Family Well-Being Plan worksheet. Think about how you might respond differently.

For each accommodation you withdraw, you have the choice of eliminating it altogether or gradually phasing it out. Rachel's decision to not wait for Sam past the designated time is an example of eliminating an accommodation. Had Rachel felt this was too difficult, she could have told Sam she'd wait ten minutes beyond the announced departure time. Although waiting ten minutes is still an accommodation, it's a big improvement over what had been happening. If Rachel's eventual goal was to eliminate waiting time altogether, she could reduce the time she waits gradually over time.

Should you stop an accommodation completely or reduce it gradually? There are two factors to consider. First, what is the impact of the accommodation on your life? The goal of step 4 is to improve your emotional well-being. That means making whatever changes are necessary to reduce the burden you've been enduring by providing accommodations. You don't always have to eliminate an accommodation completely to improve your well-being. Sometimes reducing it somewhat or changing how you provide the accommodation—say, doing it in a way that's more convenient for you—is sufficient to reduce your burden.

Second, what change are you willing to make? If you don't feel prepared to eliminate a particular accommodation altogether, you could simply scale it down. The key is follow-through. It's better to make changes you're prepared to implement than to attempt something more ambitious and not follow through. We make this point often, but for good reason.

Brainstorming how to reduce accommodations takes some practice. To help you think out options, here are some examples of partially reducing or gradually phasing out accommodations:

- If your loved one frequently seeks reassurance throughout the day: "I will meet with you at 5 p.m.—for fifteen minutes—and answer any questions as best I can. If you ask me questions the rest of the day, I will respectfully remind you that it is not 5 p.m."

- If your loved one expects you to do their laundry daily: "I will do one load of your laundry per week if it is in the green hamper designated for your clothes and the green hamper is placed in the basement next to the washing machine by Saturday at noon. I will return the green hamper to your room with your clean clothes in it that Saturday afternoon."

- If your loved one relies on you to wake them up in the morning: "If you'd like, I'm willing to make one attempt to wake you up each morning at 8:00 a.m. I will not be responsible for getting you out of bed, and I will make no further attempts to wake you up after that."

- If your loved one expects you to cook special meals for them: "We'll prepare one dinner menu for the entire family each evening. You are not required to eat the meal we prepare. However, if you want something other than the family dinner we prepare, you'll need to prepare it yourself."

- If your loved one expects you to complete their homework for them: "I'll help you, but I won't do your homework for you. I'll be available from 7 to 8 p.m. each evening to give you feedback about your homework and to answer questions. I will not be available to help you with your homework outside of the specified hour."

As you can see, there are different ways to withdraw accommodations and set limits. What you decide depends on how fast you want things to change and the pace of change you can tolerate. Whether you move slowly or quickly, the eventual objective is the same—to, as much as possible, decrease accommodations that burden you. If you choose to reduce (rather than eliminate) an accommodation, you can always decide to further reduce or eliminate it down the road. Whatever you decide, it should be something that lessens your burden and enhances your emotional well-being.

Like you, Rachel wanted to treat herself better. See how she planned to do this:

Part 2: The Solution
How I Plan to Treat You Better: I am going to refrain from lecturing you or yelling at you. I plan to talk to you gently and respectfully instead. I'll let you know that we are supposed to leave at X time. If you would like, I'll remind you an hour before it's time to leave. And I would like to have you come with me. But if you're not able to make it, I'll understand, and I won't be upset with you.
How I Plan to Treat Myself Better: If you are not ready to leave at the planned time, I will leave by myself.

Now it's your turn. What accommodations will you reduce, and what will you do instead? Write this in the "How I Plan to Treat Myself Better" row.

Almost done with your solution—you just need a start date.

Task 5: Identify a Start Date

You've reached the final step in developing your family well-being plan. In deciding when to begin, make sure you're giving your loved one sufficient time to prepare for the changes you'll make. The easier the transition for them, the less pushback you're likely to receive. And that'll make the transition easier for you. Ordinarily, we suggest giving one week's notice, but you can choose a longer or shorter amount of time if you prefer. One caution, though: if your plan includes multiple changes, consider staggering the start dates so everything doesn't begin all at once. This will be easier for everyone involved.

Rachel gave Sam one week to prepare. During the transition week, she continued to accommodate, but tried to cut back on her minimizing—the lecturing and yelling—right away. Having selected her start date, Rachel's plan was complete.

Rachel Goldberg's First Family Well-Being Plan

Part 1: The Problem
The Situation: You continue checking to make sure doors and windows are locked and appliances are off when it's time to leave the house.
How I've Been Responding: I sometimes yell at you. I tell you "We need to go now." I lecture you. I try to reassure you that nothing bad will happen while we are gone. I help you do your checking to try to get you to move faster, but I do it in a way that shows how frustrated I feel in that moment. I sometimes yell at you the next day. Later I feel guilty and apologize for overreacting.

Part 2: The Solution
How I Plan to Treat You Better: I am going to refrain from lecturing you or yelling at you. I plan to talk to you gently and respectfully instead. I'll let you know that we are supposed to leave at X time. If you would like, I'll remind you an hour before it's time to leave and that I'd like to have you come with me. But if you're not able to make it, I'll understand and won't be upset with you.
How I Plan to Treat Myself Better: If you are not ready to leave at the planned time, I will leave without you.
Start Date: I week from today.

Have you thought about how much notice you'll give your loved one? Write the date your plan will start in the "Start Date" row.

If you've filled out all five rows, congratulations! You've developed your first family well-being plan. There'll be additions to your plan later on, or new plans you'll draft in response to other parts of the family trap you want to target. But for now, focus on making this initial effort successful.

Moving Forward

As we reach the end of this chapter, your initial family well-being plan should be ready to go. That means you've identified a problematic situation, how you've been responding, how you plan to respond in the future, and when your plan will begin. Now on to chapter 12, where you'll put your plan into action.

Implementing Your Plan to Ease Family Distress

Main Point: You'll be using the family well-being plan you developed in chapter 11 to change how you interact with your loved one. You'll learn how to present your plan and how to implement and update it successfully.

If you feel apprehensive right now, you're not alone. Most families do. It's natural to wonder how your loved one will respond and whether you're up to the task. It's true, they're likely to push back when you first change how you deal with recovery avoidance. But keep in mind, you're not going to be changing everything at once. The changes you make will happen one step at a time, and that should be manageable for you both. Besides, your plan promises less minimizing, and that's usually welcome news to a family member saddled with recovery avoidance.

Let's Get Started

This is a very important moment. You'll soon be taking another step out of the family trap. It may only be one situation, one kind of problematic interaction with your loved one, but one change can build a foundation for the future. Moreover, this is an opportunity to establish your credibility—to show that you say what you'll do, and then do it. Once they learn this, future changes become a whole lot easier to implement. Get ready to say what you'll do—to tell your loved one what to expect.

Presenting Your Plan to Your Loved One

As we've indicated in prior steps, it's important to tell your loved one what you're about to do. And that means putting it in writing (see "Telling Your Loved One About the Changes You Plan to Make" for a review). If other family members have joined you, consider writing one letter representing a unified message from all of you to your loved one. You can attach all your family well-being plans to the letter. If you prefer, each person can write their own letter and attach it to their plan. It's up to you. Just be sure all the letters follow the format we've suggested. Here's the letter Rachel sent her husband, Sam:

> Dear Sam,
>
> As you know, I've been taking steps to improve our family's well-being. I realize for that to happen, I've got to change my behavior. This means treating you better and also taking better care of myself. I apologize for not having done this sooner.
>
> Attached to this letter is a family well-being plan designed to start creating a better environment for both of us. To begin my efforts, I've selected one situation that causes us distress. I've attached my plan to improve the situation. The plan describes the situation, how I used to respond, how I will treat both of us better in the future, and the date the plan starts.
>
> Thanks in advance for reading this letter and looking over the plan. I'll be glad to answer any questions.
>
> Love,
>
> Rachel

Now try writing a letter introducing your family well-being plan to your loved one. You can use Rachel's letter as a model. Feel free to edit the content or style as needed to better fit your family.

You've come a long way! It's time to meet with your loved one once again. If you think it'd be helpful, refer back to the communication guidelines provided earlier ("Telling Your Loved One About the Changes You Plan to Make") to refresh your memory before you start the meeting. When you end the meeting, reiterate the plan's start date.

Tips to Help You Follow Through

When change happens gradually, and there's less minimizing going on, the level of resistance you encounter is often manageable. Still, every family situation is different. It may not be as bad as you anticipate, but chances are some of the changes you make won't be welcomed by your loved one. For that reason, many families find step 4 the hardest to implement. Here are some tips we hope will keep your loved one's behavior from stifling your efforts:

- **Prepare to manage your feelings.** Depending on how your loved one reacts to the changes you make, you could experience a range of emotions, including fear, anger, and guilt. These feelings can be powerful and make it hard to stand your ground. Fear and guilt can make you back down; anger can provoke you to minimize. Anticipate these feelings and have a plan for how you'll deal with them: how you might keep yourself calm when you need to, how to bring the conversation back on track if it threatens to get sidetracked, and how you might put a pin in the conversation so you can resume it when everyone's calmer, if that becomes necessary. Keep in mind that when things get heated, it's almost always best to remove yourself from the situation and give everyone time to calm down.

- **Avoid power struggles**. Focus on what you can control: your own behavior. Let go of your desire to force your loved one to change. Simply change *your* behavior.

- **Be consistent**. Following through is crucial even when your loved one pushes back. Inconsistency will make things harder for you in the long run.

- **Be prepared for resistance**. You could encounter more than just verbal protest. For example, a loved one might yell, curse, slam doors, scream, or protest in ways that upset you and the rest of the family. If they try to provoke you, don't respond. This may be hard, especially when they're behaving in ways that are particularly provocative, but ignoring them is often the best option. As long as their behavior doesn't rise to a crisis level, your planned reaction should be one of calm inattention. Don't hesitate to leave the room or get out of the house if it helps to avoid conflict. You can also consult our resources page online (http://www.newharbinger.com/53134) for more information on this topic. That said…

- **Don't be surprised if things get worse before they get better.** This is called the *extinction burst*. When you change how you react to a person, especially when you've been reacting in a certain way for a long time, it takes a while for the other person to believe you won't resume your old ways. Consider the Goldbergs. Sam didn't believe Rachel would really leave without him. After all, in the past, he'd usually been able to wear her down. When Rachel first tried to follow her plan, Sam's attempts to make her feel guilty actually got worse. His voice got louder, saying more dramatic things than ever before. But Rachel stuck to her plan. Sam eventually learned that Rachel meant what she said—that she'd leave at the scheduled time without him, if necessary. His attempts to make Rachel feel guilty softened over time, and Rachel survived Sam's extinction burst. If you encounter an extinction burst from your loved one, try to stick with your plan. If you do, things should get better eventually.

- **Be willing to implement your family crisis plan when you need to.** Not only does that help ensure your family's safety, but following through with your plan is a vital part of establishing your credibility for future changes you hope to make.

- **Be willing to contact a mental health provider if needed.** If at any point you feel in over your head, consider consultation with a trained clinician. They may be able to provide the support and guidance you need to deal with the situation.

Evaluating and Updating Your Plan

A week or two after you've implemented your first family well-being plan, take a few minutes to reflect on areas of progress and difficulty. You may be tempted to start withdrawing additional accommodations, but first ask yourself a few questions:

- **Did I cut back on the minimizing as I said I would?** In other words, did you treat your loved one better, as you promised (Row 3 of your Family Well-Being Plan worksheet)? If the answer's no, take a look at what pressed you to keep minimizing. Try to identify what feelings are behind your minimizing. That's usually the culprit. Feelings are what make it hard to step away from minimizing. You might be nagging or prompting because you're afraid they'll stumble. But stumbling is a necessary part of the process. It's what motivates a person to pursue recovery. Perhaps you yell or criticize because you're angry about the burdensome accommodations you're still providing. But remember, you'll be reducing your burden with each accommodation you stop. And you've already started this process. If you can keep these points in mind, you'll be less likely to minimize.

- **Did I reduce accommodations as I said I would?** In other words, did you treat yourself better as you promised (Row 4 of your Family Well-Being Plan worksheet)? If the answer's no, please don't start withdrawing any more accommodations—not yet. Adding more to your plate now will make it even harder to follow through. Instead, try to identify what got in your way, as we recommended in step 3, and then develop a plan to address it. A common obstacle is the emergence of a crisis. If you didn't follow your family crisis plan, make a commitment to do so next time. Whatever threw you off, apologize to your loved one—identify how you fell short and pledge to do better next time. This will help repair the damage to your credibility. Remember, every time you don't do what you said you'd do, you make it harder the next time you try to set limits.

- **Has your loved one adjusted to the changes you've made so far?** By adjusted, we mean they're not openly defiant or disruptive whenever you attempt to implement your plan. They may not like the changes you've made, but there's no major protest or related drama. Even better, you're seeing some recovery behavior. If you stopped making them lunch, and now they're making themselves a sandwich, that's a healthy adjustment to the loss of an accommodation. In some small but important way, your loved one has moved toward recovery and away from avoidance. It bears repeating: When you remove accommodations, you create opportunities for your loved one to practice recovery behavior. If they've not adjusted to the changes you've made so far, you probably just need to give it more time. Adjusting to change takes longer for some people than others.

If you answered no to any of these three questions, please pause before discontinuing additional accommodations. You may need more time to work on reducing your counterproductive behavior; your loved one may need more time to adjust to the changes you've made. Either way, now is not the time to complicate your family well-being plan. You'll know you're ready to start withdrawing more accommodations when you can answer yes to all three questions.

Rachel Goldberg was ready. She'd successfully implemented her first family well-being plan. Sam had adjusted to Rachel's new policy about leaving the house, and the conflict they once had about it was mostly absent. Encouraged by the success of her first plan, Rachel was eager to tackle another problem:

Rachel Goldberg's Second Family Well-Being Plan

Part 1: The Problem

The Situation: You ask me for reassurance that the dog is going to be OK. If I ask you to wait until later, because I am busy with something, you insist that I stop what I'm doing and talk to you immediately. And you continue asking me to answer the same or similar question over and over again until you feel satisfied.

How I've Been Responding: I've answered your questions whenever you asked them, but I'm clearly frustrated and upset. I sometimes raise my voice or talk down to you. I raise my hands in frustration. I sometimes yell "Just stop it!" through clenched teeth.

Part 2: The Solution
How I Plan to Treat You Better: I intend to be respectful when we interact. That means trying to be patient and respectful in my words and tone of voice.
How I Plan to Treat Myself Better: I'll be willing to meet with you at a planned time, each day, for fifteen minutes. I'll listen patiently and answer your questions gently, to the best of my ability. After fifteen minutes, I will stop.
Start Date: In one week.

Do you have other problematic situations you'd like to address? We suspect you do. If you've successfully implemented your first family well-being plan, return to chapter 11 and repeat the five tasks necessary to develop another plan. When the plan is done, return to this chapter to help you implement it. You can repeat this process until you've addressed all the problematic situations important to you.

How Do You Know It's Time to Move to Step 5?

First, let's be clear when it's *definitely not* time to move to step 5: when there's still a significant level of distress within the family. Steps 3 and 4 are designed to enhance your well-being and ease family distress, which creates a family atmosphere conducive to focusing on the recovery behavior you hope to promote in step 5. When you and your loved one are stuck in a pattern of conflict, it's harder to motivate their recovery behavior without minimizing, and they're more likely to resist anything positive you try to initiate. So before moving on to step 5, make sure you've embraced valued activity and reduced accommodating and minimizing as much as possible. You'll be more effective in creating a recovery-friendly environment if you do.

Moving Forward

You may be eager to move on to step 5. But don't rush. Following through with your plan to decrease accommodating and minimizing is an important part of taking care of yourself and your family. It takes time and effort to eliminate all the counterproductive behavior that's kept you trapped. You may need several months, and sometimes much longer, to implement step 4 adequately. The time it takes depends on the number of problematic situations and the number of obstacles you encounter along the way. If it takes longer than you'd hoped, try to remain patient and persevere. Don't forget the ultimate objective—to improve your family's well-being. When your family is no longer stuck wrestling with recovery avoidance, and your loved one is no longer locked in battle with you and other family members, you'll be ready to move forward. That's when the conditions will be right to create a recovery-friendly environment. And that's what you'll do in step 5. If you're still not sure, the precheck for step 5 will help you determine whether you're ready. Good luck!

Create a Recovery-Friendly Environment

An incentive is a bullet, a key; an often tiny object with astonishing power to change a situation.

—Steven Levitt

Precheck: Do I Need Step 5?

You need step 5 if: (1) You're *satisfied* with the progress you've made with your life (steps 1–4) *and* (2) you're *dissatisfied* with the progress your loved one has made.

You might skip step 5 if: (1) You're *satisfied* with the progress both you and your loved one have made. In this case, you might not need to do anything. If applicable, you can ask their clinician how to best support their continued recovery.

or (2) You're *dissatisfied* with the progress both you and your loved one have made. In this case, revisit steps 1 through 4 and try to determine what went wrong. Chapter 15 may help you determine whether you need something beyond the five steps featured in this book.

or (3) You're *satisfied* with your loved one's progress but *dissatisfied* with your progress. In this case, it may be helpful to see a health care professional who can help you identify the problem and address it. Something other than your loved one's condition may be affecting your emotional well-being.

Risks of skipping step 5: You'll have missed an opportunity to encourage recovery behavior in your loved one.

If you skip step 5: Continue to monitor your family's progress. If the situation changes, consider trying step 5 at that time.

CHAPTER 13

Developing Your Plan to Create a Recovery-Friendly Environment

Main Point: You'll learn concepts and strategies designed to encourage your loved one to engage in recovery behavior. You'll develop an incentive plan that includes the specific behavior you want to promote, the incentives you'll use, and how you'll gauge whether your efforts are succeeding.

Take a moment to congratulate yourself. Most families work hard to get to step 5. It takes a lot of patience and perseverance to get this far. We hope that your family's situation has improved and that you feel the effort has been worth it.

So far (steps 1 through 4), the focus has been on changing your behavior. To do that successfully, you had to stop trying to change your loved one, at least for a while. In step 5, you'll resume trying to influence your loved one, but the difference now is in how you'll go about it. You won't be lecturing, nagging, or pressuring them to change. Instead, you'll be creating an environment that promotes recovery.

Let's Get Started

By recovery-friendly environment, we simply mean one that actively promotes the development of recovery behavior. You've already begun to do this. Every time you stopped yourself from accommodating, you created an opportunity for your loved one to learn a new behavior. Each time you resisted the urge to minimize, and instead spoke to them with compassion and respect, you helped create a world in which they are more likely to feel understood and less likely to avoid recovery. In step 5, you'll take things to another level.

You'll be strategically incentivizing recovery. If all of this isn't crystal clear yet, read on.

Let's start with a brief review of the relationship between consequences and behavior.

Consequences Affect Behavior

- Things that happen after behavior occurs are called consequences.

- Consequences can influence the future occurrence of a behavior.

- Positive consequences make a behavior more likely to occur.

- Negative consequences make a behavior less likely to occur.

Simple, right? A child at a recital is more likely to sing a second time if the initial performance is greeted with applause and less likely to do so if met with ridicule. The inclination to seek the positive and avoid the negative determines a great deal of human behavior, including whether one pursues or avoids recovery.

As you completed steps 1 through 4, you may have already witnessed the power of consequences. You probably saw changes in your loved one's behavior after you changed your behavior. That's because the changes you made created new consequences for them, and the right consequences are an important part of an environment that promotes recovery behavior. Remember the Garcia family? When Sara and her daughter stopped managing Gabriel's food intake, he experienced the natural consequence of hunger. That influenced Gabriel to feed himself, and that's a recovery behavior—a small step toward becoming self-sufficient.

There's a difference, though, between what you've done so far and what you'll do now. The steps you've completed so far weren't meant to modify your loved one's behavior, but to improve your well-being by changing your behavior. That doesn't mean the changes you made didn't influence your loved one; they almost certainly did. But the influence was incidental—meaning it wasn't the primary goal of your effort. In step 5, the changes produced in your loved one won't be incidental, but rather a direct result of the incentives you create.

Using Incentives to Change Behavior

The strategic use of consequences to influence behavior is called *incentive management* or contingency management. An incentive, or reward, is a positive consequence used to encourage behavior; a disincentive, or penalty, is a negative consequence used to discourage behavior. Incentive management uses incentives and disincentives to promote behavior change. It's your best option to foster recovery behavior in your loved one because it uses things within your control. You can't control the beliefs, skills, or goals of people who are unreceptive, but you can create incentives and disincentives to influence their behavior. That's in your control. You can create positive consequences (incentives) to reward recovery behavior, or you can create negative consequences (disincentives) to penalize recovery avoidance.

We'll guide you to work with both, but we strongly prefer the use of positive consequences whenever possible. Negative consequences are more likely to escalate family distress and are much more difficult to follow through with. Moreover, positive consequences help you steer clear of power struggles. As Benjamin Franklin said, you can catch more flies with honey than with vinegar.

Developing Your Incentive Plan

Putting your plan together involves seven tasks:

1. Identifying behaviors you want to target

2. Selecting the target behavior you want to incentivize first

3. Defining the target behavior precisely

4. Deciding how you'll track that target behavior to make sure it's happening

5. Selecting an incentive you believe will be effective

6. Deciding what amount of incentive to award

7. Determining how you'll administer the award

Please don't skip over any of these tasks; they're all essential. We'll be using Olivia's family, the Robinsons, to illustrate how this works. Recall that Olivia's brother, Robert, has OCD. We'll show you how Robert's parents developed an incentive plan. Their first task was to decide which recovery behaviors they wanted to promote.

Task 1: Identify Target Behaviors

A target behavior is the specific behavior you're going to try to increase. The following list includes recovery behaviors commonly targeted by families trying to promote positive change in their loved one, sorted into three categories.

RECOVERY BEHAVIORS

Seeking Professional Help:

- Explore resources to find a therapist or psychiatrist.

- Contact a clinician, make an appointment.

- Attend a session with a clinician to be evaluated.

- Meet with a psychiatrist.

- Take medication prescribed by a psychiatrist or other physician.

- Meet regularly with a therapist.

- Complete therapy homework assignments.

Seeking Other Kinds of Help:

- Read a book or article about a relevant problem.

- Gather information from credible sources.

- Attend a support group that promotes recovery.

- Attend a relevant lecture, conference, or event.

- Communicate with someone with a similar problem.

Making Improvements in Functioning:

- Assume a new responsibility (chores, projects).

- Apply for a job, volunteer work, or school.

- Go to work, volunteer, or attend class.

- Learn and practice a new skill (driving, cooking, managing money).

- Engage in self-care and hygiene (proper sleep, exercise, eating).

- Interact with others (family events, social activity).

- Pursue a hobby, sport, or other special interest.

Which of these behaviors are relevant to your loved one's needs? Which do you hope to see them develop? If you think of any behaviors not on the list, feel free to include them, as long as they represent a step toward recovery and are things you value.

Task 2: Select Your First Target

Next, you'll select which behavior(s) you'd like to target first. It's generally advisable to start with just one or two behaviors. It might be tempting to tackle more than that, but overly ambitious plans are more difficult to implement and less likely to succeed. Zeroing in on one or two will be easier for you and your loved one. You can target additional behaviors later.

Deciding where to begin can be difficult. The target behavior you select depends largely on your loved one's specific pattern of recovery avoidance. Understandably, some families are eager to initiate treatment as soon as possible. This might be feasible for a recovery avoider who's at least considered getting help in the past. But for someone who's persistently refused treatment, it might be difficult to find an incentive powerful enough to make this happen right away. If your loved one is clearly unwilling to consider getting help, unless you can create a very powerful incentive, aim for a less ambitious target to begin with.

An alternative is to target improvements in functioning, like taking on household chores or attending a class online. These may feel more doable to a loved one who's been refusing treatment. If treatment's not an option now, try not to be too discouraged. It can happen down the road. Start with modest goals and introduce more challenging targets over time. Sometimes a loved one's resistance to treatment lessens as functioning improves.

If your loved one's already receiving treatment but not benefiting, consider targeting behavior that might improve outcome. The target you select depends on why you think your loved one's not getting better. If you believe the wrong treatment is being provided, you can incentivize seeing an alternative provider, one that you approve of. If, on the other hand, you believe they're getting the right treatment but not participating enough to make a difference, you can encourage them by offering incentives to keep their session appointments, supporting them in completing therapy homework. or getting more family involved.

After you've given it some thought, select the behavior(s) you're going to target first. If you're still having trouble deciding, seek input from other family members or a mental health professional. Be careful not to do too much at once. Think of your incentive plan as a work in progress, one that you'll update over time. Remember, this is only the beginning. The plan doesn't have to be perfect, and you don't have to anticipate everything that might happen. You'll be able to update any aspect of the plan as you go.

Task 3: Define the Target

The behavior you want to target needs to be defined. A useful definition describes what the behavior looks like and when and where it needs to take place. That gives you and your loved one a shared understanding of what must occur for an incentive to be awarded.

The Robinsons recognized the strength of Robert's opposition to treatment, so they selected a less ambitious initial target: reading about OCD. This is how they defined the behavior:

Behavior	
What:	Robert will read the book *Overcoming OCD*
When:	4 to 5 p.m. every day
Where:	At the dining room table

Note how clearly the Robinsons defined their target behavior. Now it's time for you to do the same. You can use the Incentive Plan worksheet at http://www.newharbinger.com/53134. Fill in the first three rows as the Robinsons did, then move on to task 4.

Task 4: Decide How You'll Track the Target

To administer incentives effectively, you need to know whether the target behavior has occurred. That means establishing a system for tracking the behavior, including who'll be doing the tracking.

Most of the time, the tracker is either you or your loved one, although sometimes another person like a relative or a clinician can be involved. An important consideration is the extent to which you feel your loved one's report can be trusted. You could ask them to fill out a daily or weekly log to document when they've completed a target behavior. That's less work for you and provides another opportunity for your loved one to practice recovery behavior. However, if there's reason to suspect their reliability, you may need to be the tracker. In that case, it's preferable that you witness the behavior as it occurs or have valid evidence the behavior has happened.

The Robinsons had concerns about Robert's reliability, so they wanted him to read in a location where his behavior could be observed. His mother decided to be the tracker. In the fourth row, "How we'll keep track," they wrote down exactly how she'd do it:

Behavior	
What:	Robert will read the book *Overcoming OCD*
When:	4 to 5 p.m. every day
Where:	The dining room table
How we'll keep track:	Mom will enter a checkmark on the kitchen calendar on each date the behavior occurs.

You've seen the Robinsons' tracking system. Now decide how you'll track the target behavior you've selected. Enter the information in the row provided on the Incentive Plan worksheet.

You're now finished with the target behavior. Next, you'll decide which incentive to use.

Task 5: Select an Incentive

Before you make your selection, it's important to understand that incentives are more effective when they are

- **Valued and desired by the recipient.** The incentive you select needs to reflect your loved one's general preferences and interests. For example, a reward of Brussels sprouts is unlikely to incentivize someone who hates vegetables. Also remember, an incentive should be administered when there's desire or need for it. Food is a far more effective incentive when someone's hungry.

- **Awarded after the behavior is performed.** Incentives should be awarded only after the target behavior has occurred. Do not award incentives based on the promise of behavior—that would teach your loved one that they can obtain the incentive without having to engage in the target behavior.

- **Within your control.** Whatever incentive you select, it should be within your control. Money might be a powerful incentive, but it's irrelevant if you can't afford to provide it.

- **Distributable in increments.** The incentive should be awardable in small amounts for small samples of behavior. That way, if your loved one fails to earn the incentive today, there'll still be incentive to try again tomorrow. For that reason, avoid using all-or-nothing incentives. Offering a trip to Disney World for a good report card would be an all-or-nothing incentive. A more effective incentive would be offering X amount of time to play video games based on Y amount of time spent studying that day. Earning points toward a trip to Disney World might be incentivizing for the right person, but for many, receipt of the reward would be too far off in the future. And that violates the next criterion for an effective incentive.

- **Awarded soon enough to incentivize the behavior.** Delayed rewards are less effective. It's best if the incentive is awarded immediately. However, a weekly schedule can be effective and is more practical if it's too cumbersome to administer rewards daily. If you use a weekly schedule, you can use points or tokens that can be awarded daily but cashed in at the end of the week.

- **Consistently awarded based on clearly defined conditions.** Be clear about what the reward is and what your loved one must do to receive it. Being consistent is important. If your loved one loses confidence that the incentive will be received, they'll be less willing to engage in the target behavior.

We realize it can be challenging to find an incentive that meets all of these criteria. But try to find one that meets as many as possible. The incentive doesn't have to be perfect, just good enough. To help you think this out, here are the incentives most often used by the families we work with:

Money is a versatile motivator because it can be used to obtain something each individual finds personally rewarding. The main downside, of course, is the cost. Some families simply can't afford the amount of money it would take to influence meaningful recovery behavior. We also realize some people might oppose using money on philosophical grounds. Perhaps you feel as if you'd be buying your loved one's compliance; that using money would dehumanize them, or that you shouldn't have to pay someone to do something "they should be doing anyway." We understand these feelings, but before you decide, please consider this: There are only a few useful incentives that you might have control over. If you elect not to use money and you can't find another useful incentive, what then? You'll have limited options. You could, of course, employ disincentives to penalize recovery avoidance, but we've already cautioned you about the downside of using negative consequences. After that, the only option you'd have left is returning to the tactics of prodding and other forms of minimizing, something we don't recommend.

Think of financial incentives as a recovery allowance—a fund that supports the pursuit of improvements in functioning. At the end of the day, an incentive is simply a positive consequence used to encourage behavior—and often, once a behavior occurs, additional positive outcomes arise that can serve as additional reinforcers. Which is to say, if you use money to spur recovery behavior now, the behavior that money is incentivizing might create opportunities to experience additional incentives. Take Vijay, for example. He's a recovery avoider with a severe bridge phobia. Vijay's parents are using money to incentivize him to practice driving over bridges. When he makes it to the other side, he's likely to discover other reasons to continue crossing bridges.

Time spent in a rewarding activity is an option that may be more realistic for some families, particularly for those with financial limitations. Parents, for example, can create an opportunity for their teenage child to earn access to the family car or an electronic device by engaging in a specified recovery behavior.

Time spent with a rewarding person capitalizes on the potential value of time spent with others. Of course, your loved one must enjoy the company of whoever is used as the incentive. Examples of this option include a young child who earns special time with Mommy or Daddy or a grandparent incentivized to earn extra time with the grandkids. Ordinarily, the incentive would be granted over and above normal family time.

Point systems are a little different from the first three incentives; they are *symbolic* incentives. Each point represents some amount of the real incentive, which is usually one of the three incentives already described. Points and tokens can be awarded immediately and cashed in for the real reward at a later, more convenient time.

Once you've chosen the type of incentive you're going to use, you'll need to determine how to create the incentive. We'll use a hypothetical Video Game X to illustrate three options:

- **Offering access to something new.** Example: Parents purchase Video Game X and provide opportunities for their child to earn playing time. This option works nicely when the chosen incentive is not currently accessible to the child.

- **Offering bonus access to something familiar.** Example: Parents allow their child to earn extra time on Video Game X. This option is feasible if access to the incentive is currently limited, and the child desires additional playing time.

- **Converting something familiar from open access to restricted access.** Example: Parents stop allowing unrestricted access to Video Game X and require their child to earn playing time. This option is necessary when a loved one currently has unlimited access to the incentive, and no other novel incentive can be created.

One caution here: Be prepared for resistance if you use option 3. People don't like to lose something they're used to having, even when given the opportunity to earn it back. For that reason, options 1 and 2 are typically easier to implement. You'll get more pushback from your loved one with option 3. That said, in some family situations, options 1 and 2 just aren't feasible. Sometimes option 3 is the only way to create an effective incentive.

The Robinsons used option 1 (providing access to something new) to create an incentive, and they chose money to incentivize Robert to read.

Robert was unemployed and had no allowance or other source of income. He also liked to collect vinyl records, so there was reason to believe the opportunity to earn money would be incentivizing.

What incentive did you select? Don't enter it on the Incentive Plan worksheet just yet. First, you need to decide the amount of each award.

Task 6: Decide the Amount of Incentive to Award

Having selected the incentive, you'll need to determine the amount you'll award for each occurrence of the target behavior; how many minutes, dollars, or points your loved one will receive each time the behavior happens.

In making your decision, ask yourself

- *What can I realistically afford (time, money, effort)?*

- *What do I think will motivate my loved one?*

The first answer should be relatively easy to determine. You probably know how much time you're willing to spend or the amount of money you can afford. The second question is a bit trickier. You'll have to rely on what you know about your loved one and make your best guess. You can always up the ante if your initial amount wasn't enough. The Robinsons chose $10, an amount they could afford and that they believed would influence Robert.

Now think about the amount of incentive you'll use. Write this in the "Amount" row.

You're almost done; just one more task to complete.

Final Task: Decide How You'll Award the Incentive

It's usually helpful to have a designated time the incentive will be awarded and a set interval between incentive awards (daily, weekly). Try your best to follow reliably whatever method you decide upon. The Robinsons didn't want the inconvenience of managing cash, so they decided to transfer money directly into Robert's bank account. They didn't want the hassle of having to administer awards daily, so they chose to deliver the incentive once a week. Here's what the Robinsons' incentive plan looked like with all the sections completed:

Behavior	
What:	Robert will read the book *Overcoming OCD.*
When:	4 to 5 p.m. every day
Where:	The dining room table
How we'll keep track:	Mom will enter a checkmark on the kitchen calendar indicating each date the behavior occurs.
Incentive	
Amount	$10
How it'll be awarded:	Each Friday at 5:00 p.m., Mom will check the calendar, calculate Robert's earnings for the week, and deposit the money in his checking account.

How will you award the incentive you've selected? Enter it in the "How it'll be awarded" row.

Nice work! Your initial incentive plan is done.

Moving Forward

Hopefully, at this point you've completed all six rows of your Incentive Plan worksheet, specifying the behavior you're targeting, the incentive you'll use, the methods for tracking behavior change, and how you'll award the incentive. In the next chapter, you'll start putting your plan into action.

CHAPTER 14

Implementing Your Plan to Create a Recovery-Friendly Environment

Main Point: In this chapter, you'll put your incentive plan into action. You'll learn how to present the plan to your loved one, how to avoid common pitfalls, and how to revise your plan as you go along.

You're about to implement your first Incentive Plan. The principles provided in this chapter will help you do so successfully. Do your best to follow your plan as you said you would. That helps establish credibility for later attempts to promote recovery behavior in your loved one.

Let's Get Started

As you implement your incentive plan, be careful not to fall into old patterns. Making the switch from changing *your* behavior to trying to change *your loved one's* behavior can be difficult. The counterproductive behavior you worked hard to leave behind can easily creep back into interactions with them. We'll try to keep you on top of this as you implement your plan.

Presenting the Incentive Plan to Your Loved One

Before telling your loved one about the incentive plan you've developed, it's helpful to review the general communication guidelines provided earlier ("Telling Your Loved One About the Changes You Plan to Make"). As always, you'll begin by writing your loved one a letter, like the one the Robinsons wrote to Robert:

Dear Robert,

As you know, we've been taking steps to improve the well-being of our family. Our initial efforts were to improve the quality of our lives. Now we'd like to do something for you, to help ensure you a better future. Our goal is to help you develop the skills you need to be self-sufficient.

Attached is an incentive plan we developed. The plan describes what behavior will be rewarded, what the reward will be, and when and how you'll receive it.

We have no intention of bugging you about this. Your participation is entirely voluntary. If you choose not to participate, that's of course your choice. We simply want to provide the opportunity.

The opportunity to earn rewards will start a week from Monday. Thanks in advance for reading this letter and looking over the incentive plan. Please let us know if you have any questions.

Love,

Mom and Dad

Now it's time for you to write your letter. Use the Robinsons' letter as a model. Feel free to edit the content or style as needed to better fit your family.

After you've written the letter, attach your Incentive Plan worksheet and set up a meeting with your loved one. Run the meeting as our guidelines suggest. As always, do your best to avoid minimizing, and try to stay out of power struggles. Remember, let the letter express your thoughts, with the conversation serving as reinforcement of the plan.

Transitioning to the Incentive Plan

The two weeks following your meeting are a period of transition. The first week provides an opportunity to help you and your loved one prepare for the changes that are coming. During this time, you can rehearse implementing the plan. For example, you might start getting in the habit of checking the tracking log at the designated time. You can also provide reminders to help your loved one prepare for the week ahead. Each day at 4:00 during the transition week, for instance, Ms. Robinson reminded Robert "This time next week you'll have the opportunity to earn money by reading."

The first week you're implementing the incentive plan is also a week of transition. The plan has started, but things aren't routine yet. For the first couple of days, it may be necessary to remind your loved one about the plan. You can even place visual reminders in places where your loved one will see them—as Mr. Robinson did when he placed a copy of *Overcoming OCD* on the dining room table where he knew Robert would notice it.

Monitoring the Plan

As you oversee your incentive plan, keep the following tips in mind:

- **Be careful.** Don't overdo the reminders and prompts. Your loved one needs to learn how to do this themself. And reminders can easily be experienced as pressure and turn into minimizing.

- **Be patient.** Try not to get overinvested in what happens on a given day. Give the incentives time to work. Some individuals don't respond to an incentive until they've repeatedly failed to earn the reward and are convinced it will be awarded only when the target behavior occurs. And if your loved one happens to miss a day or more, don't overreact; change is hard, and the most important thing is to stay committed to the plan overall.

- **Be tolerant of failure.** Again, allow your loved one to stumble. Change isn't easy, and failure to earn a reward today can increase motivation to earn it tomorrow. When your loved one doesn't appear to be responding to the incentive, it may be tempting to nudge or lecture or prompt them—but try not to. We hope by now we've convinced you of the counterproductive effects of minimizing.

- **Be consistent.** Never give a reward that hasn't been earned; always award it when it *has* been earned.

- **Be reliable.** Follow through with the plan as you said you would. It'll be less effective if your loved one begins to doubt the plan's credibility.

- **Be flexible.** You can change your plan from week to week if it isn't working the way you'd hoped. But always notify your loved one ahead of time of the changes you'll be making.

Evaluating and Updating Your Plan

Remember, your initial incentive plan is just that—your initial plan. Almost every plan needs to be revised eventually, often multiple times. How you modify the plan depends on whether your loved one is engaging in the behavior you targeted.

If the targeted behavior *isn't* happening, you have two options:

- **Target a less challenging behavior.** Consider this option when you suspect the initial target was overly ambitious. If the Robinsons determined that reading was too difficult for Robert, they could select a less challenging initial target, like listening to an audiobook.

or

- **Enhance the incentive.** Consider this option if you believe the amount of the incentive is too low. For instance, if the Robinsons felt $10 didn't generate enough incentive for Robert to keep up with his reading, they could raise the amount to $15.

If the target behavior *is* happening, you also have two options:

- **Retain the initial target:** Consider this option if you're satisfied with your loved one's level of functioning. For example, if the initial target was to attend therapy sessions, and they're attending sessions as hoped, no further changes may be indicated. You might even decide to discontinue the incentive plan if they're making progress in therapy and seem to be independently motivated to continue.

or

- **Change the target to something more challenging.** Consider this option when you'd like to reward a higher level of recovery behavior.

The Robinsons' initial incentive plan worked. Robert successfully finished reading *Overcoming OCD*. But that wasn't the end goal. The Robinsons wanted to focus on a more challenging target—incentivizing Robert to take medication. At the same time, they wanted to promote Robert's self-sufficiency skills, so he was rewarded only if he took the medication without being prompted by his parents. Any day his parents had to prompt him, he got no reward for that day. Here's what the new plan looked like:

Behavior	
What:	Robert will take his medication as prescribed without being prompted by his parents.
When:	In the morning before noon
Where:	In the kitchen
How we'll keep track:	Each morning, Mom either will watch Robert take his medication or will check the pill dispenser at noon. If Robert has taken his medication, without prompting, Mom will put a checkmark on the calendar.
Incentive	
Amount	$15 per day
How it'll be awarded	Each Friday at 5:00 p.m., Mom will check the calendar, calculate Robert's earnings for the week, and deposit the money in his checking account

It might be helpful to see other examples of an incentive plan. Here's how other families you've read about in this book tried to promote recovery behavior in their loved ones:

- Sara Garcia decided to incentivize Gabriel to attend family events. For every family gathering he attended without protest, Sara promised to prepare one of Gabriel's favorite dishes for his next meal.

- Vivienne Chen wanted to get the clutter out of Mei's dining room so her kids could someday eat dinner safely at their grandmother's house. Each week, for every box of things Mei took out of the dining room, Vivienne offered Mei an extra hour with the grandkids on the weekend. Family visits had to take place somewhere other than Mei's home, however, at least until Vivienne was convinced her mother's home is safe.

- Cathy Martin implemented a "recovery allowance" to encourage Caitlyn to contribute more to the household. Cathy made a schedule that described one daily household chore (cooking dinner, cleaning the bathroom, and so on) for each day of the week. Caitlyn received $10 for every chore she completed by the designated time. Like the Robinsons, Cathy wanted to foster her daughter's self-sufficiency, so Caitlyn was rewarded only if the target behavior was performed without being prompted by Cathy.

- Rachel Goldberg wanted to use Sam's love of jazz to incentivize him to get treatment. Sam missed going to concerts. Rachel didn't like jazz, and Sam was too nervous to go alone. For each therapy session Sam attended, Rachel offered to attend one musical performance. Until Sam was further along in his therapy, Rachel was willing to help him with his checking rituals to ensure they made it to the concert on time.

Moving Forward

You now know how to put together and implement an incentive plan. Now let's see how the recovery avoider in your life responds. We hope everything goes smoothly, but there could be bumps in the road. Don't worry; this is normal. When it happens, simply revisit chapter 13 and modify your plan, then implement it following the guidelines provided here. There are many ways to change an incentive plan—you can target new behavior, increase the strength of the incentive, use an entirely new incentive, or change how the incentive is awarded. Hopefully you'll discover a plan that moves your loved one in the right direction. If you succeed, congratulations! If not, and you're confident you've given your plan enough time to work, you may need to consider the options presented in chapter 15.

Other Steps You May Consider

Main Point: You'll learn three additional steps some families contemplate when dealing with recovery avoidance. We'll help you decide whether one or more of these steps is right for your situation.

You've learned the five main steps of the family well-being approach. If you're satisfied how things have turned out, congratulations! You've completed your journey out of the family trap. But if you feel further change is needed, you may find this chapter helpful. We'll present three additional steps to consider: (1) removing a foundational accommodation, (2) getting professional consultation, and (3) planning for the road ahead. It's good to know about each of these, but they're not for everyone. Take your time and consider each one carefully.

Removing a Foundational Accommodation

Again, foundational accommodations provide a loved one with the basics of life, like shelter, food, and health care. Withdrawing this kind of accommodation can be a powerful intervention, but it also comes with significant risk. No longer allowing your loved one to live in your home is an example of discontinuing a foundational accommodation. It's easy to see the risks involved.

Removing a foundational accommodation may remind you of "tough love," a well-known intervention that allows loved ones to experience the consequences of their behavior. In one sense, our approach is similar. When you stop accommodating, you're allowing your loved one to experience the consequences of recovery avoidance. However, tough love is sometimes used to describe interventions that are incompatible with our approach, like authoritarian parenting or the discipline used at boot camps for troubled adolescents. With an emphasis on the word "tough," these approaches often include minimizing—criticism, yelling—and aren't compatible with family well-being. As we'd predict, research suggests strategies like this are often ineffective and can make things worse (Flett et al. 2013; Wilson, MacKenzie, and Mitchell 2005).

There's another type of tough love, however, one with a greater emphasis on the word "love." Proponents like Bill Milliken advocate a firm but compassionate approach to people avoiding recovery (Milliken and Meredith 1968). Accommodations are discouraged because they're viewed as enabling the individual's unhealthy behavior. That's the "tough" part. At the same time, families are encouraged to avoid minimizing, to speak with empathy and kindness even when their loved ones challenge them. That's the "love" part. This second kind of tough love is more compatible with our approach. In fact, you were practicing something similar as you worked your way through the steps already outlined. Withdrawing accommodations while refraining from minimizing is what healthy tough love is all about—love that allows you to set boundaries to ensure the well-being of the family as a whole, love that means doing whatever's possible to promote your loved one's recovery. And at times, tough love could include removing a foundational accommodation.

Up until now, we've cautioned you about the risks of discontinuing foundational accommodations. Removing such basic levels of support can rapidly accelerate conflict within the family and jeopardize your loved one's safety. Furthermore, families often struggle with follow-through, and this hinders the credibility of any future attempts to set limits. That said, despite the risks, there are circumstances in which you might consider it.

When to Consider It

There are two situations in which to consider discontinuing foundational accommodations: when your family's safety or basic welfare is threatened, or when you're unable to create a positive consequence that works.

WHEN YOUR FAMILY'S SAFETY OR BASIC WELFARE IS THREATENED

Sometimes continuing to provide a foundational accommodation places the family in harm's way. That can include threats to person, property, or the family's financial stability. In such situations, a foundational accommodation may need to be discontinued to protect the rest of the family. A loved one who threatens to injure other family members might need to be removed from the household. A family struggling to make ends meet might have to stop paying for a loved one's living expenses. In both examples, removing a foundational accommodation was necessary to protect the family's safety or basic welfare.

WHEN YOU CAN'T CREATE A POSITIVE CONSEQUENCE THAT WORKS

For some families, step 5 is not an option. They're simply not able to create the kinds of incentives necessary to promote recovery behavior. Take, for example, using money as an incentive. A recovery avoider with a generous trust fund is unlikely to be influenced by financial incentives. And money may not even be an option for families with limited income. For other families, the problem is difficulty monitoring behavior change. For example, if a recovery avoider lives in one state and their family lives in another, it may be impossible to reliably track whatever progress is occurring.

The bottom line is that some families simply have no realistic way to create an incentive plan powerful enough to generate recovery behavior. And in those cases, nothing short of removing a foundational accommodation—like financial support, food, or shelter—may provide the necessary incentive to reverse recovery avoidance.

If this is your dilemma, you face a difficult decision. If you remove a foundational accommodation, you must live with the risks involved. If you avoid the risks, you must give up the one thing left in your control that might promote your loved one's recovery. You could resume minimizing, but you know how well that works. For some families, removing a fundamental accommodation might be the only feasible option. If you're considering it, there's more you need to know.

What to Know Before Proceeding

Remember chapter 8? We alerted you then to the risks of removing a foundational accommodation. If you go this route, you must be willing to (1) let your loved one deal with the challenges of survival without the accommodations you've withdrawn, and (2) endure whatever guilt and apprehension arise along the way. You must also be willing to handle your loved one's response. There's likely to be resistance—not just from your loved one, but also from other family members. None of this is easy.

Here are a few things you can do to help you make the choice and follow through:

- **Be sure you have a solid reason to do this.** Stopping accommodations out of anger or frustration is not a solid reason. You're unlikely to follow through. Think this out. Make sure you're doing it for one of the two reasons we've detailed.

- **Consider modifying your plan to reduce risk.** Are there safer ways to achieve the same end? For example, if, for whatever reason, you no longer want your loved one at home, can you afford to pay the rent for an apartment? You'd still be providing a foundational accommodation, but under safer conditions.

- **Assemble a support network.** It helps to have the ear of others who understand. Find out which family members and friends are on board. This is especially helpful if there are unsupportive or critical family members. The more members who can present a united front to the loved one and to resistant family members, and support each other when things get tough, the better.

- **Be prepared for crises.** They're likely to happen. Hopefully, you addressed this in step 1. If not, return to chapters 5 and 6, put a family crisis plan together, and be prepared to implement it.

- **Be good to yourself.** Your guilt and self-doubt may lead to self-criticism. It's important to catch yourself when you're doing this. Dealing with recovery avoidance is difficult for everyone involved, including you. You deserve compassion, not criticism. Treat yourself with kindness. You're likely to need it.

- **Don't hesitate to use the resources available in your family.** If you're apprehensive about your loved one's survival, maybe there's someone you know who could shoulder the burden of caring for them, at least for a while. If you're asking your loved one to leave your home, is there someone other than you—an ex-spouse, a brother or sister, a grandparent, an aunt or uncle—who could house them?

- **Take advantage of other resources.** In addition to friends and family, there may be other sources of support for your efforts. Do some research. Are there agencies, support groups, chat rooms, and the like that might be helpful? This includes getting professional consultation.

If you're about to remove a foundational accommodation, be sure to follow our suggestions. You'll probably need them all. Getting professional consultation is especially important. That's the next step for you to consider.

Seeking Professional Consultation

It's smart to seek expert advice when you need it. If you've got a legal problem, you find a lawyer. If you're struggling with financial issues, you hire an accountant. Why should it be any different when the problem is recovery avoidance? Dealing with a loved one who's avoiding recovery is one of the most challenging problems a family can face. The right mental health clinician might be able to give you the guidance you need.

Qualified mental health clinicians include psychologists, licensed clinical social workers, professional counselors, marriage and family therapists, psychiatric nurse practitioners, and psychiatrists. Not all states in the US have the same licensing laws, so you'll need to do some research to determine which professionals are licensed to practice in your state. If you live outside the US, check the licensing laws in your country.

When to Consider It

Consider seeking a professional's help if you've had difficulty pursuing family well-being on your own. Perhaps you struggled with trying to develop the plans needed for steps 1 through 5. Maybe you developed your plans but didn't follow through with them. Or you followed through for a while but couldn't keep it up.

Remember those obstacles we mentioned in chapter 4, the ones that can sabotage your success? They can interfere with your ability to implement the changes you want to make. A competent mental health clinician might help you identify and overcome these obstacles. Some people just need guidance in following the steps. Others may need time to address their own issues before they're emotionally and mentally prepared to deal effectively with their loved one.

What to Know Before Proceeding

In an ideal world, you'd work with someone with expertise in recovery avoidance. The resources at http://www.newharbinger.com/53134 include a list of clinicians trained in the family well-being approach. We're working hard to train more clinicians, but, regrettably, the list is still too short to help all the families who need it.

If you're unable to work with one of the therapists on the list, you still have options. Most therapists knowledgeable about behavior change and family issues should be able to help you, especially if they're willing to use our book as a guide. Here are a few tips to help direct your search for the right therapist:

- **Find a family specialist.** Look for clinicians who list "family therapy" or "family consultation" among the services they provide.

- **Or find someone who specializes in your loved one's problem.** If your loved one has received an official diagnosis and you know what it is, you can look for an appropriate specialist. For example, if your loved one has social anxiety, find a clinic or provider that specializes in social anxiety disorder. Some therapists work regularly with their patients' families and may be willing to work with you, even if your loved one doesn't participate. But be sure the therapist understands that you're seeking someone to help you change your behavior; specifically, how you interact with your loved one.

- **Or find a clinician who uses CBT or other behavioral approaches.** CBT is a therapeutic approach that focuses on behavior change and emphasizes practical solutions to problems. In that sense, clinicians who use CBT should be comfortable with the kinds of interventions used in the family well-being approach. Look on the therapist's website for terms like "behavior therapy," "cognitive behavioral therapy (CBT)," "cognitive therapy (CT)," "acceptance and commitment therapy (ACT)," "dialectical behavior therapy (DBT)," "problem-solving therapy," "behavioral activation," "exposure therapy," or "exposure and response prevention (ERP)." These are different forms of CBT.

- **Consider your first contact with the therapist a test run.** Think of it as a job interview for the therapist. You're under no obligation to return for a second visit if you're unconvinced a particular clinician can help you. And don't hesitate to get a second or third opinion if you feel it would be helpful.

- **Be prepared to hear "There's nothing I can do."** Many therapists are used to working only with an identified patient and may have little or no experience working with their families. If so, helping you instead of your loved one may be a foreign concept for them. If they say there's nothing they can do unless your loved one wants help, move on. They don't have the perspective necessary to assist you.

- **Be clear about what you're looking for.** When you first speak with the therapist or the therapist's intake office, tell them you want a clinician to help you deal more effectively with a recovery avoider. If they're unfamiliar with that term (they may well be), tell them you want to become less "codependent" or to learn "how to stop enabling a loved one."

- **Assess the clinician's willingness to use this book.** When you speak with therapists, mention this book and ask them specifically if they'd consider using it as a guide to help you.

- **Visit relevant websites.** Go to the websites of professional or advocacy organizations that promote evidence-based treatments—treatments validated by scientific research. Many of these organizations have directories that list therapists from different areas of the US and other countries. There's a list of website addresses of some of these organizations at http://www.newharbinger.com/53134.

- **Explore resources outside your region.** With the expansion of telehealth and changes in laws regulating interstate delivery of care in the US, you may have access to some professionals who practice outside your local area. You'll need to check local, state, and national regulations.

- **Try not to let financial limitations stop you.** We understand there are many obstacles to finding affordable healthcare, but there may be agencies or community clinics in your area that provide free or low-cost services. Similar services are sometimes available at universities that offer a degree in one of the mental health disciplines. Contact colleges in your area to see if one has a training clinic with low-cost care accessible to the public.

If you've struggled to make headway with the recovery avoider you love, advice and support from a mental health professional might be what you need. Establishing a working relationship with a therapist can help you both now and later as issues arise, which will help you navigate the road ahead.

Planning for the Road Ahead

You don't have to be dealing with recovery avoidance to think that planning for the future's a good idea. Trust funds, life insurance, savings accounts, and retirement plans are all examples of preparing for the road ahead. Planning for the future is, in part, being prepared for the things you can't predict. But it's also about anticipating the challenges you know you're likely to experience, such as medical issues, a decline in mobility, and financial constraints. When your loved one is a recovery avoider, there's another set of challenges you might have to prepare for.

Have you thought about how your loved one might function in the world without the assistance you currently provide? The sad truth is, we're all mortal. There's no guarantee you'll always be around to help. You may need to consider the financial, legal, social, medical, and psychological issues to be addressed to ensure your loved one's future welfare. If you haven't yet, now's the time. It never hurts to be prepared for things to come.

When to Consider It

The necessity for a long-range plan depends on how well your loved one is doing. If they're functioning well, you might decide it's unnecessary to develop a plan, or at least that it's no longer your responsibility to do so. But what if they continue to struggle? Without treatment, most psychiatric disorders don't improve and can worsen over time. We know this can be difficult to accept, but you might need to prepare for the possibility that their condition may never improve. Remember the Stephen King quote from step 1? Let's hope for the best, as we prepare for the worst.

To help you decide whether you need a plan for your loved one's future, ask yourself:

- Do they have a reliable source of income (stable job, trust fund, pension), or are they taking steps (coursework, training) to obtain a reliable source of income that would enable them to live independently?

- Do they have the skills (ability to manage finances, problem solve, communicate with others, and so on) necessary to live independently?

If you answered no to either of these questions, we strongly recommend that you plan for the future. Before you begin, there are some key things to know.

What to Know Before Proceeding

If you've held off planning for the future, it's understandable. There are lots of reasons to avoid the topic. It's not particularly pleasant to think about, and you might not even know where to begin. We're here to help you get started. We'll identify the issues you should consider and point you toward helpful resources. Depending on your loved one's needs, a useful plan might need to address finances, legal issues, housing, transportation, health care, social support, activities of daily living, and advocacy and problem-solving.

FINANCES

Financial resources are important to the success of any long-term plan. You'll need to estimate the costs of housing, food, transportation, insurance, medical care, and other necessities. Then you'll need to estimate the available funds: trusts, government benefits, job income, and other income sources. Many families find it helpful to work with financial planners and attorneys. For instance, a family might pursue a power of attorney to have someone assigned as a financial spokesperson for their loved one. Another family might secure an estate planning attorney who can set up a third-party special-needs trust to support accessing (and retaining) services.

Consider looking into government sponsored supports such as Social Security Disability Insurance (SSDI) or Supplemental Security Income (SSI). You may want to consult with a financial planner or attorney for advice on obtaining and retaining these benefits.

LEGAL ISSUES

Legal resources may be needed to support your financial goals. A lawyer with the proper expertise can help you evaluate and pursue options like guardianship/conservatorship, power of attorney (for medical decisions), and wills and trusts.

HOUSING

Your loved one will always need a place to live. The options included in your plan depend on their ability to live independently. If they are self-sufficient, independent living might be possible. If not, other options include living in another family member's home, an apartment with a caregiver who makes home visits, or a more structured environment like assisted living.

TRANSPORTATION

How will your loved one get from place to place? Is driving a car an option? Is there a public transportation system where they'll be living, and are they capable of navigating the system? Taxi and ridesharing services are another option. Maybe a family member or friend can help out. Your loved one might also qualify for paratransit curb-to-curb services like Call-A-Ride.

HEALTH CARE

Access to health care is an important part of any life plan. And that means, in part, insurance. Perhaps your loved one is already covered by Medicare or Medicaid. If not, will they have enough financial support to obtain insurance through a government program like the Affordable Care Act? Do you have other options for ensuring that they have adequate coverage? Who will make sure they get to doctor visits and take medication as prescribed?

SOCIAL SUPPORT

Your loved one's need for social support is another consideration. Who will provide the interpersonal, spiritual, and recreational support important for their quality of life? Will they have contact with family, friends, or neighbors? Are they part of a religious community that can provide support? There are also service organizations that address the social needs of impaired individuals.

ASSISTANCE WITH ACTIVITIES OF DAILY LIVING

Consider the extent to which your loved one needs assistance with basic self-care. Will they be able to maintain proper hygiene, get dressed each day, do laundry, eat properly, empty the trash, and so on? Family members might be willing to help somewhat, but encourage them to be realistic. They should be careful not to overcommit.

ADVOCACY AND PROBLEM SOLVING

Problems arise from time to time that need to be addressed—pipes break, tires go flat, roofs leak, and so on. Will your loved one be capable of handling all of this? If not, who will do it? Will a family member assume this responsibility? Will someone need to be hired? Who'll advocate for your loved one when needed?

In this section, we've touched on issues to consider when planning for your loved one's future. It's not within the scope of this chapter or our expertise to touch on everything necessary to develop a comprehensive plan, but hopefully we've given you a place to start. You can also check out the resources at http://www.newharbinger.com/53134. There's more information there and links to additional resources as well.

Moving Forward

Our goal has been to improve your family's well-being. We hope you're better off now than before you read this book. If everything's not quite the way you'd hoped, don't give up. As long as there's something new you haven't tried, there's reason to keep trying. And whatever you do, remember the serenity prayer. Focus on the things in your control. If you hope to influence others, start by changing your own behavior. That's the key to family well-being—the alternative to waiting on, pleading with, or vainly hoping for your loved one to change. It's your way out of the family trap. If you're not there yet, we hope that with patience, persistence, and a willingness to return to the steps of the family well-being approach—you'll get there someday.

Six Examples of Living in the Family Trap

The Garcia Family

Sara Garcia's forty-five-year-old husband, Gabriel, has battled depression for many years, but his condition has worsened considerably since taking medical leave from his job two months ago. Gabriel sleeps most of the day and watches television late into the evening. He's withdrawn from his friends and feels too ashamed to let visitors in the house. Gabriel rarely helps out around the house and doesn't feel ready to return to work. Sara and her seventeen-year-old daughter Ana have assumed all of the household responsibilities, stopped attending church activities they used to enjoy, and no longer have friends over to visit. Their efforts to motivate Gabriel have been unsuccessful, and they're tired of trying to cheer him up. He refuses to seek treatment because, he says, "it won't do any good." They try to be understanding but are increasingly resentful that Gabriel doesn't do anything to help himself or the family. Sara worries that her salary as a librarian may not be enough to make ends meet and they might have to sell the house.

The Robinson Family

Stacy and Steve Robinson are a married couple concerned about Robert, their twenty-two-year-old son. He has severe OCD and has become disabled by his worries about contamination. Robert washes his hands over eighty times a day and gets upset when others touch anything that belongs to him or that he has to touch. The Robinsons' fourteen-year-old daughter, Olivia, has been significantly affected by her brother's OCD. She's not been able to have a friend come to her house for over a year because Robert "will have a fit," and Stacy and Steve haven't had friends or family in their home since Christmas two years ago. Robert's unable to attend school or get a job, but he refuses to seek help. He insists that his parents do everything he asks of them and becomes extremely upset if they don't comply exactly with his demands. Robert once threw a chair at his parents because they refused to change their "contaminated" clothing. The Robinsons are intimidated by what Robert might do if they don't comply with his demands. In an effort to appease Robert, Stacy has stopped exercising and rarely socializes with friends. Steve finds himself increasingly angry and irritable, frequently raising his voice and snapping at Robert, something that's out of character for him. Steve's irritability is negatively impacting his relationship with Stacy and Olivia, as well as with Robert.

The Chen Family

Vivienne, Amy, and Andrew Chen are the adult children of Mei, who has a hoarding problem. Vivienne lives in the same town as their mother, but Andrew and Amy live hundreds of miles away. Mei Chen's disorder has never been formally diagnosed, but the problem is evident. There are stacks of clutter piled as high as the ceiling in almost every area of her house. The only places without clutter are Mei's bed, a very small area of the kitchen, and just enough space in the bathroom to use the toilet. Vivienne visits weekly and repeatedly pleads with Mei to part with some of her possessions, but Mei refuses. The three children once tried to "clean out Mom's place" while Mei visited a friend for the weekend. When Mei returned, she was furious and accused her children of stealing from her. Amy and Andrew are furious with their mother for running up huge bills on the credit card they gave her, and they visit Mei only once a year, during the Chinese New Year. Vivienne still visits regularly but feels Mei's home isn't safe for the grandchildren. The situation has become urgent because Mei's home has been condemned by the city inspector.

The Martin Family

*Cathy Martin is a single parent concerned about the disruption that
social anxiety has caused in her fifteen-year-old daughter's life. Caitlyn
is hypersensitive to criticism and dealing with questions about her sexual
orientation. She fears being judged by others in their small town and
feels misunderstood by everyone, including her mother. Cathy is most
worried about the number of days Caitlyn's missed school and the
amount of time she spends online. Cathy arranged for Caitlyn to see a
therapist, but after one visit, Caitlyn claimed the therapist didn't
understand her. Instead of asking for a different clinician, Caitlyn
refused any further therapy, proclaiming "It's stupid." Since Caitlyn's
anxiety makes it difficult for her to be alone, Cathy seldom leaves the
house. She used to get up early to walk and prepare for work; now she
spends hours each morning begging her daughter to go to school,
reassuring Caitlyn that other people aren't judging her. Cathy feels
overwhelmed and alone. Cathy is unwilling to air her "dirty laundry,"
and she feels like a failure because she can't hold her family together.*

The Polanski Family

*Roy and Lynn Polanski have been married for twenty years. Roy and
his two daughters are upset about the family disruption caused by
Lynn's unresolved physical complaints. Over the past ten years, she's
experienced various episodes of fatigue, pain, and bowel-related distress.
Each episode results in extensive medical attention. Lynn spends several
hours a day researching potential causes for her symptoms and posting
updates about her physical condition on social media. Physicians have
been unable to determine a definitive cause for Lynn's symptoms.
Treatments sometimes work temporarily, but whatever benefit she
receives never seems to last. Roy takes time off from work to accompany
Lynn to physician visits and pays for her many hospitalizations and
medical tests. Her daughters are tired of responding to Lynn's medical
emergencies without any apparent progress and are bothered by Lynn's
absence from most family functions because of her illness. When*

psychotherapy is suggested, Lynn becomes defensive, accusing her family of insinuating that she's "making it all up" and insisting that the doctors "just haven't found the right diagnosis yet."

The Goldberg Family

Rachel and Sam Goldberg have been married for forty-two years. Sam was diagnosed with OCD when he was in high school; after a couple of unsuccessful medication trials, he was prescribed a medicine that seemed to work well for a while but eventually stopped being effective. For the last three years, Sam and his psychiatrist have tried several different medications, but none have been effective. Rachel and the doctor have been encouraging Sam to seek therapy for his OCD, but he refuses. He continues to argue that there "must be" a medicine that will help him "get back to my old self." The Goldbergs don't have children, but they do have a dog they describe as their "furry baby." As part of his OCD, Sam worries he'll be responsible for harm coming to the dog, to Rachel, or to their home. To deal with his fear, Sam "checks," over and over again, to make sure doors and windows are locked, appliances are turned off, and no items are left out that could hurt the dog. Sam seeks reassurance from Rachel throughout the day, asking her to answer the same questions over and over again until he feels reassured. This is a major source of stress for Rachel. Sam's compulsions take up much of his day, and he often requests Rachel's help in order to stop. Leaving the house is especially hard for Sam. Rachel is sometimes hours late to appointments, or misses them altogether, because of the assistance she provides Sam.

Glossary

Accommodation (or accommodating): Any behavior that aids, satisfies, or compensates for an impaired individual's special needs or requests. Under normal circumstances, it can provide useful assistance to a person attempting to accomplish tasks or complete goals. However, when provided to someone who's avoiding recovery, accommodations can worsen impairment and elevate family distress. Negative effects of accommodating include eliminating opportunities for the impaired individual to practice recovery behavior, lessening their motivation to seek recovery, and burdening the family members who provide the accommodation.

Accommodations of commission: The extra responsibilities or adjustments in routine that a family member adopts in response to the limitations or demands of an impaired individual. These are things the family member typically wouldn't do for a person who isn't impaired. They're also things the recovery avoider could benefit from doing. Examples include doing your child's homework, assuming your spouse's household responsibilities, repeatedly providing reassurance, or walking on eggshells to avoid upsetting someone.

Accommodations of omission: The valued activities you drop or neglect to pursue because of the demands of dealing with an impaired individual. Personal time once devoted to the pursuit of normal life goals and fulfillment is spent monitoring or assisting an impaired individual. Examples include no longer entertaining guests at home, giving up favorite leisure activities, and quitting a job.

Counterproductive behavior: Any action that hinders family well-being and promotes recovery avoidance. The two types of counterproductive behavior relevant to families dealing with a recovery avoider are the acts of accommodating and minimizing.

Family trap: The dysfunctional family environment that develops when one or more family members respond to a loved one's recovery avoidance by accommodating and minimizing. The more the family accommodates and minimizes, the more the loved one avoids recovery. And the more the loved one avoids recovery, the more the family accommodates and minimizes. It's a vicious cycle of increasingly higher levels of impairment, chaos, drama, conflict, and distress for everyone involved.

Family well-being approach: A therapeutic intervention to help families dealing with recovery avoidance, including five steps developed by the authors to help families escape the family trap:

- Preparing for crises
- Redefining the problem
- Embracing valued activity
- Easing family distress
- Creating a recovery-friendly environment

Family well-being consultation: The service provided by mental health clinicians when using the family well-being approach to assist families to escape the family trap.

Foundational accommodation: An accommodation of commission that provides the basic necessities of life, like food, shelter, or health care. The risks involved in withdrawing a fundamental accommodation are high, so it should be considered only under certain circumstances.

Minimization (or minimizing): Persistent, ineffectual behavior intended to influence an impaired individual to change. It's called minimizing because the behavior conveys a lack of appreciation for the challenges experienced by an individual avoiding recovery, implying that the individual can change because of something the minimizer says or does. Examples include lecturing, nagging, yelling, pleading, criticizing, prodding, and any other behavior designed to get impaired individuals to do something they're unable or unwilling to do.

Problematic situation: Any interaction involving conflict between a recovery avoider and other family members; most often, it's when the recovery avoider's impairment interferes with the lives of other family members.

Productive behavior: Any action that enhances family well-being and promotes recovery-compatible behavior; the opposite of counterproductive behavior.

Recovery avoidance: Persistent failure to explore, pursue, or take advantage of resources and opportunities available for resolving problems or improving health or functioning. It refers to physical or mental activity that blocks progress toward purposeful, personal life goals. This is a common human response that has particularly serious consequences when the level of impairment is severe.

RA: Abbreviation for recovery avoider, a person who engages in recovery avoidance.

Recovery behavior: Any act consistent with the pursuit of improved health or functioning or the resolution of problems. Recovery behavior is the opposite of recovery avoidance.

Situational accommodation: An accommodation of commission that is limited to a specific situational challenge; for example, doing an individual's laundry or driving an individual to the store. In contrast to a foundational accommodation, situational accommodations are less risky to discontinue because the consequences of doing so typically don't threaten the basic safety or welfare of the impaired individual.

References

Butzlaff, R. L., and Hooley, J. H. 1998. "Expressed Emotion and Psychiatric Relapse: A Meta-Analysis." *Archives of General Psychiatry* 55: 547–552.

DeCou, C. R., Comtois, K. A., and Landes, S. J. 2019. "Dialectical Behavior Therapy Is Effective for the Treatment of Suicidal Behavior: A Meta-analysis." *Behavior Therapy* 50: 60–72.

Fekadu, W., Mihiretu, A., Craig, T. K. J., and Fekadu, A. 2019. "Multidimensional Impact of Severe Mental Illness on Family Members: Systematic Review." *British Medical Journal* 9: 1–20.

Flett, M. R., Gould, D., Griffes, K. R., and Lauer, L. 2013. "Tough Love for Underserved Youth: A Comparison of More and Less Effective Coaching." *Sports Psychologist* 27: 325–337.

Hooker, S. A., Masters, K. S., Vagnini, K. M., and Rush, C. 2019. "Engaging in Personally Meaningful Activities Is Associated with Meaning Salience and Psychological Well-Being." *The Journal of Positive Psychology* 15: 821–831.

Lebowitz, E. R., Marin, C., Martino, A., Shimshoni, Y., and Silverman, W. K. 2020. "Parent-Based Treatment as Efficacious as Cognitive-Behavioral Therapy for Childhood Anxiety: A Randomized Noninferiority Study of Supportive Parenting for Anxious Childhood Emotions." *Journal of Child and Adolescent Psychiatry* 59: 362–372.

Lebowitz, E. R., Panza, K. E., and Bloch, M. H. 2016. "Family Accommodation in Obsessive-Compulsive and Anxiety Disorders: A Five-Year Update." *Expert Review of Neurotherapeutics* 16: 45–53.

Linehan, M. M., Heard, H., Clarkin, J., Marziali, E., and Munroe-Blum, H. 1993. *Dialectical Behavior Therapy for Borderline Personality Disorder.* New York: Guilford.

Milliken, B., and Meredith, C. 1968. *Tough Love.* Old Tappan, NJ: Revell Co.

Pollard, H. J., and Pollard, C. A. 2002. "Someone I Care About Is Not Dealing with His OCD: What Can I Do About It?" *OCD Newsletter* Summer: 1–5.

—————. 2006. "Families of OCD Sufferers Seldom Get the Help They Need: Why They Don't and Why They Should." *OCD Newsletter* Spring: 14–15.

Shimshoni, Y., Shrinivasa, B., Cherian, A. V., and Lebowitz, E. R. 2019. "Family Accommodation in Psychopathology: A Synthesized Review." *Indian Journal of Psychiatry* 61: S93–S103.

Stein, A. T., Carl, E., Cuijpers, P., Karyotaki, E., and Smits, J. A. J. 2021. "Looking Beyond Depression: A Meta-Analysis of the Effect of Behavioral Activation on Depression, Anxiety, and Activation." *Psychological Medicine* 51: 1491–1504.

Substance Abuse and Mental Health Services Administration (SAMHSA). 2022. *Key Substance Use and Mental Health Indicators in the United States: Results from the 2021 National Survey on Drug Use and Health* (HHS Publication No. PEP22-07-01-005, NSDUH Series H-57). Rockville, MD: Center for Behavioral Health Statistics and Quality, SAMHSA.

VanDyke, M., Pollard, C. A., Harper, J., and Conlon, K. E. 2015. "Brief Family Consultation to Families of Treatment-Refusers with Symptoms of Obsessive-Compulsive Disorder: Does It Impact Family Accommodation and Quality of Life?" *Psychology* 6: 1553–1561.

Wearden, A. J., Tarrier, N., Barrowclough, C., Zastowny, T. R., and Rahill, A. A. 2000. "A Review of Expressed Emotion Research in Health Care." *Clinical Psychology Review* 20: 633–666.

Wilson, D. B., MacKenzie, D. L., and Mitchell, F. N. 2005. "Effects of Correctional Boot Camps on Offending." *Campbell Systematic Reviews* 1: 1–45.

Real change *is* possible

For more than forty-five years, New Harbinger has published proven-effective self-help books and pioneering workbooks to help readers of all ages and backgrounds improve mental health and well-being, and achieve lasting personal growth. In addition, our spirituality books offer profound guidance for deepening awareness and cultivating healing, self-discovery, and fulfillment.

Founded by psychologist Matthew McKay and Patrick Fanning, New Harbinger is proud to be an independent, employee-owned company. Our books reflect our core values of integrity, innovation, commitment, sustainability, compassion, and trust. Written by leaders in the field and recommended by therapists worldwide, New Harbinger books are practical, accessible, and provide real tools for real change.

C. Alec Pollard, PhD, is founding director of the Center for OCD & Anxiety-Related Disorders at Saint Louis Behavioral Medicine Institute, and professor emeritus of family and community medicine at Saint Louis University School of Medicine. He is a licensed psychologist with a special interest in the study and treatment of individuals with anxiety and emotional disorders who refuse or otherwise fail to benefit from evidence-based treatment. Pollard, codeveloper of the family well-being approach (FWBA), has authored or coauthored more than one hundred publications and leads the Family Consultation Team at Saint Louis Behavioral Medicine Institute.

Melanie VanDyke, PhD, is a licensed psychologist at the US Department of Veterans Affairs, and the Center for OCD & Anxiety-Related Disorders at Saint Louis Behavioral Medicine Institute. She was awarded Missouri Psychologist of the Year (2023) and has authored research articles and educational materials for professionals, patients, and families. VanDyke was principal investigator for the family well-being consultation research project, and is codeveloper of FWBA.

Gary Mitchell, LCSW, is a senior staff clinician at the Center for OCD & Anxiety-Related Disorders at Saint Louis Behavioral Medicine Institute. He is a licensed clinical social worker specializing in the treatment of children and adults with obsessive-compulsive disorder (OCD), anxiety disorders, and related problems. He is an original member of the Family Consultation Team at Saint Louis Behavioral Medicine Institute, and codeveloper of FWBA.

Heidi J. Pollard, RN, MSN, is currently in private practice where she consults with families dealing with a treatment-reluctant loved one. She was an original member of the Family Consultation Team at Saint Louis Behavioral Medicine Institute, and a codeveloper of FWBA.

Gloria Mathis, PhD, is co-owner of the Mid-Atlantic Center for OCD & Anxiety in Columbia, MD. She is a licensed psychologist specializing in OCD, anxiety disorders, and body-focused repetitive behavior (BFRB) disorders in individuals of all ages. While completing her postdoctoral fellowship, Mathis received training in FWBA from the Family Consultation Team at Saint Louis Behavioral Medicine Institute.

Foreword writer **Gail Steketee, PhD**, is a professor and cochair in the department of clinical practice at the Boston University School of Social Work. She is coauthor of *Buried in Treasures*.